THE LIFE STRATEGIES WORKBOOK

THE LIFE STRATEGIES WORKBOOK

Exercises and Self-Tests
to Help You
Change Your Life

PHILLIP C. MCGRAW, PH.D.

NEW YORK

Designed by Ruth Lee

ISBN 0-7868-8514-9

FIRST EDITION

10 9 8

CONTENTS

PART IV: GET GOING—CREATING YOUR STRATEGY FOR THE LIFE YOU WANT

Based on Chapters 13 and 14 of Life Strategies: Doing What Works, Doing What Matters

ABOUT THIS WORKBOOK

Books don't change people. People change people. If you have any doubts about this fact of life before beginning this workbook, I hope you'll shed them once and for all. You clearly hope for a better life, and you've taken a first step toward it by acquiring *Life Strategies: Doing What Works, Doing What Matters* and the companion workbook. Everything you'll find in these books is based on the presumption that you have within you every trait, tool, and characteristic necessary to create a quality life; you are simply not maximizing them.

It's time to roll up your sleeves and get to work, taking an unvarnished look at you—no masks, no cons, no squeamishness. Get real with yourself, for yourself. The knowledge and assignments you'll find in these books will help you evaluate everything in your life based on whether it's working or not—whether you are getting results you want or getting results you don't want. Truth and clarity about yourself and your life will give you access to power you've never imagined. Getting real with yourself is a foundational process that will help you emerge with strength.

This workbook is designed to help you apply the critical

life knowledge presented in *Life Strategies: Doing What Works, Doing What Matters.* I intend to provide you with a formula for success. It's not about willpower, not about intentions; it is about action, courage, and commitment. Right now, I'm offering you one of the best opportunities you'll ever get to have the life you want. But to *have* different, you'll need to *be* different and *do* different. You will gain only as much as you're willing to invest. You can help yourself by:

> stopping all of the dishonesty and self-deception that has caused you to misdiagnose yourself and your life—*get real;*
>
> acquiring the relevant knowledge and power that comes from learning the ten Life Laws set forth in *Life Strategies,* these intractable laws that govern your life and everyone else's—*get smart;*
>
> preparing yourself in knowledge, spirit, and behavior to create different results in your life—*get ready;*
>
> becoming goal-and-action oriented in every important aspect of your life—*get going.*

If you do the work on the following pages, you'll gain a new level of objectivity as you put into writing what you need to know about yourself. You'll stop blaming others and take responsibility for your life. You'll recognize that if it gets better, it will be because you make it get better. You'll teach yourself what no one ever taught you about having a successful life. I suggest that if you complete the challenges and assignments in this workbook, you will come to really know yourself for the first time in your life. You are creating an opportunity to have a truly intimate relationship with yourself.

I don't promise that every ill in your life will be cured or that everything you want will fall into your lap. But if you do the work, I can assure you that you will become a stronger, wiser, and abler manager of the only life you've been given. Life Law 1 states that *You Either Get It, or You Don't,* and now I'm telling you, you either want it, or you don't. This is all about getting what you want out of your life.

PART I

GET REAL

*Facing the Truth
about Yourself*

Before you begin this portion of the *Life Strategies Workbook*, read the introduction and Chapter 1: "Get Real," of *Life Strategies: Doing What Works, Doing What Matters*.

Whether you're curing an illness, fixing a malfunctioning machine, or improving a faulty design, the first thing you must do is figure out what isn't working and why. This is just as true for your life as for your health, your car, or your business. The exercises in this section of the workbook are designed to help you take a completely honest look at what your life is like right now, why it is as it is, and how you got there. This information will help you later as you conduct the "Guided Tour of Your Life" in Part III of this workbook.

In this and all of the work ahead, you'll be asked to put your observations, thoughts, and plans *in writing*. I can't emphasize enough the importance of this. Writing things down gives you a level of objectivity you need if you're going to be, do, and have different in your life. Do *all* of the exercises, and give them your best attention and effort. The more thorough and specific you are now, the more effective you'll be later in putting the ten Life Laws to work for you.

A QUICK SELF-CHECK   Think of this as an exercise that's roughly equivalent to checking for "where it hurts." You'll do this much more specifically after giving some time and attention to bringing yourself up to date on your life so far. However, you already know what some of the pressing problems in your life are. Read the following list and put a check mark beside any items that sound like your present experience. In the spaces provided, add any item(s) that you know need attention right now.

_____ I'm frustrated that I am not making more money in my job or career.

✓____ I'm capable of more than I am accomplishing.

✓____ I'm stuck in a rut and not getting what I want.

_____ I'm bored with myself.

_____ I'm silently enduring an emotionally barren life or marriage.

_____ I'm trudging zombie-like through a dead and unchallenging career.

✓____ I'm consistently failing in the pursuit of my goals.

✓____ I'm just "going through the motions" of my life with no passion, no plan, and no goal.

√ I'm living in a fantasy world in which I think I'm bullet-proof, when in fact my actions entail incredible risks.

_____ I'm living in a comfort zone that yields too little challenge and too little of what I do want, and too much of what I don't want.

_____ I'm living a lonely existence with little hope for change.

√ I'm suffering financial burdens I can't handle.

√ I'm living with lingering guilt, frustration, or depression.

_____

_____

_____

THE STORY OF MY LIFE

You've taken a quick look at what isn't working in your life. But how did you get here? As you go through Part II of this workbook and gain a deeper understanding of the Life Laws, you will want to identify times and ways in which the Life Laws have always been at work in your past and present life. In order to gain the greatest insight and understanding as you study the Life Laws, lay the groundwork now by writing "The Story of My Life."

Begin by creating a chronology in time-line form. You'll find a sample time line below that you can use as a model for creating your own time line on a separate piece of paper. In order to make this as clear and useful as possible, you may want to break the record of your life into chronological pieces as follows: Childhood; Adolescence; Young Adulthood; Married or Adult Life; and Later Life. In the boxes above the time line, you should record any events that you feel shaped you in positive ways. In the boxes below the line, record those events that shaped you negatively. Select only those key events that relate to who you have become today, using a few summary words to describe each event. Be as honest and fair as you can.

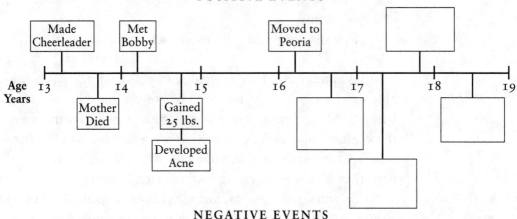

SAMPLE TIMELINE
Adolescence

Now write a narrative history. Don't worry about style, grammar, or vocabulary. Just tell your story as though you were speaking to an old and trusted friend. You may find it more revealing and helpful to tell it by the five strands that you will examine and use when you create your life strategy later: "My Personal Life History"; "The History of My Relationships"; "My Professional History"; "My Family History"; and "The History of My Spiritual Experience." As you write, emphasize these elements:

Your earliest childhood memories
How you felt in comparison to your peers as you were
    growing up
Your first significant achievement; your first memorable
    failure
Key events in your childhood home
Key events in your school experience
First key events in your dating life

Your first heartbreak and why it happened
How you chose your career/work
How you chose your life partner or chose not to have one
Your significant spiritual experiences, both positive and negative
Key successes and failures in each strand of your life

Whatever you have carried with you from the past probably carries significance for you. Whatever you think a special friend needs to know about you matters to you. Furthermore, those events and experiences that you *remember to hide* from others have importance in your life. Make these a part of the narrative. You'll be referring to them later.

As you write the story, include your feelings about all of the events you choose to record. We are not looking for a dispassionate chronology of your life, but rather one that describes what happened, why it happened, and how you felt about it. If an event or series of events in fact changed your life, say so and explain why and how. Describe both your motives and your reactions. If a certain action you took caused your first guilt feelings, note it. If certain things happened in your life that you attribute to luck, it's important that you say so; likewise, say if you feel that divine intervention is responsible for events in your life, if you feel that you behaved in a self-destructive way, were victimized, or were falsely accused. These emotional details will become the "spice in the soup" of your life story. Be thorough and be honest. If you are ashamed, say so; if you are proud, claim that pride.

"WHAT THE HELL WAS I THINKING?" You've just relived some of the most formative times in your life. In retrospect, what choices did you make or what behaviors did you choose that you now know were incredibly stupid? Describe at least five specific examples of bad scenarios. Record

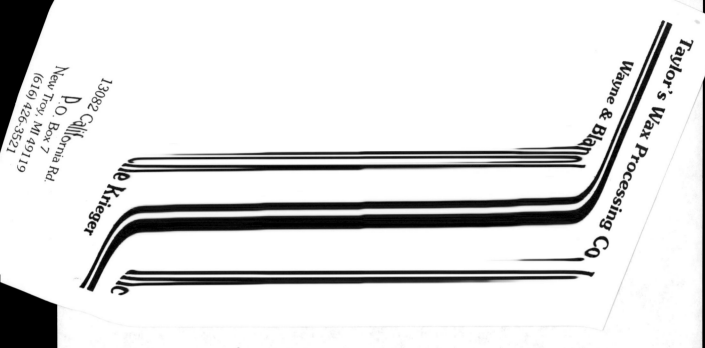

Taylor's Wax Processing
Wayne & Bla... Co

...e Krieger

13082 California Rd.
P.O. Box 7
New Troy, MI 49119
(616) 426-3521

2.

3.

4.

5.

**MY FAMILY
LEGACY**
It's almost impossible to overemphasize the influence that your upbringing has on your choices and behavior as an adult. That's why in Texas, we have a saying: "You have to rise above your raising." I'm not talking about blaming your childhood for your own bad choices in adulthood. But if you're going to get real about how you're living and why you're living that way, you need to recognize how much you have carried with you from your childhood models—how much you mimic the ones who raised you—often without even realizing it. You've been programmed like a computer, but you may have been programmed with misinformation.

Now, this exercise will require that you use some real memory muscles. If your parents or other influential people from your childhood are still living, you will have to lay aside the present people and relationships in order to thoroughly recall your impressions, emotions, and reactions as a child literally in their power. In other words, you may have a relationship with a parent that has matured into a healthy, present-day friendship, but that defined you differently in earlier times. You must ignore any present good feelings for the moment. This is critically important, because those childhood experiences live on, whether or not you recognize that they do. Identify the flaws and fallacies of your parents. You can only "rise above your raising" if you give yourself permission to criticize the ones who raised you.

Begin with your father or father-surrogate.

1—Write a *complete physical description* of your father. Include size, shape, coloring, characteristics, typical gestures, posture, and mannerisms. Describe his face, eyes, hands, and feet. What did he smell like? What did his voice sound like? Describe his favorite chair, his typical activities, the tilt of his head, or the tip of his chin. Insofar as you're able, re-create him before your eyes.

Having now re-created your father in your mind, answer questions 2 through 8 with all the candor and honesty that you can muster. Again, it is not disloyal to give your honest feelings a voice. Even if they are not feelings of which you are particularly proud, they are your feelings, and you are entitled to them. Once you have answered these questions, move on to question 9.

2—What I hate about my father is:

3—What I wanted from my father that I did not get was:

4—What I got from my father that I did not want was:

5—What I resent about my father is:

6—What I love about my father is:

7—What my father gave me that I will always value and treasure is:

8 — The behaviors, choices, or qualities of my father's that I am mimicking in my own life and relationships are:

9 — Write a letter to your father. After you've written it, you don't have to mail it. You can do whatever you want with it. Put it away, burn it, keep it nearby to look at it again— it's up to you. The point is to get in touch with the effect that this person had on you and the legacy you've carried into your present life from him. As you write the letter, be honest about your feelings. Tell your father how you feel and why. Tell him what he has done to you and for you. Most importantly, give yourself permission to give your feelings a voice in this letter.

Now repeat the exercise with your mother or mother-surrogate.

1 — Write a *complete physical description* of your mother. Then answer the rest of the questions with that mental and emotional image firmly before you.

2 — What I hate about my mother is:

3 — What I wanted from my mother that I did not get was:

4 — What I got from my mother that I did not want was:

5 — What I resent about my mother is:

6 — What I love about my mother is:

7 — What my mother gave me that I will always value and treasure is:

8 — The behaviors, choices, or qualities of my mother's that I am mimicking in my own life and relationships are:

9 — Write a letter to your mother, using the same guidelines as those for your letter to your father.

If your childhood included other significant familial relationships (that is, grandparents, siblings, or other adult family members who lived with you or regularly had you "in their power"), repeat this exercise with each one.

EMOTIONS THAT TRAP ME You've now done what you needed to do in order to look over your life in some detail. You've also revisited the profound effects your parents and most significant adult family members had on you; you've reviewed the "raising" you will need to "rise above." Go back to "The Story of My Life" and the letters to the significant parent or adult figures in your life, and circle everything you wrote that reflects an emotional response. This will help you complete the following four assignments and give you a clearer view of the emotional makeup you have acquired over the years.

1 — List the *hurts* that were visited upon you throughout your life that have confined you—in other words, that have held you prisoner in ways that someone who has not suffered these violations does not experience.

2 — List the *angers* that bind you to past negative experiences and to past or ongoing relationships. As long as you are carrying these strongly negative emotions in your present life, you are allowing them to rob you in the present and future of a full and satisfying life. So pin them down by including the events and people on which your anger focuses.

3 — List the areas in your life in which you are allowing *pride* to keep you stuck in your current rut. Perhaps you are unwilling to make a helpful change because to do so would require that you admit you are wrong or that you made a mistake. Maybe you refuse to be the one who starts the dialogue in a dysfunctional relationship because you believe you're *not* the one who is wrong, and to make the first step might imply otherwise. This sort of false pride can create a powerful barrier to honesty and constructive action. Identifying the ways in which false pride is impeding you is the first step to moving beyond it.

4 —Identify your *fears*. Before you can generate strategies for eliminating, minimizing, or managing your fears, you have to exercise the courage to name them. Are you afraid of failure? Write it down. Are you afraid of being abandoned? Add it to the list. Are you afraid that others will judge you? Reject you? Laugh at you? Are you afraid of success? Whatever your fears, face them now by acknowledging their hold on your life. Describe each fear as thoroughly and specifically as possible. Then play the "what if?" game. Imagine each of those fears actually becoming reality. Write it out and play it to its logical conclusion.

For instance, suppose you are living in fear that your partner in life will abandon you. This fear may make it hard or impossible for you to fully express your love for that person or to fully enjoy the love you receive. Write in detail what would happen if in fact the person left you, for whatever reason. How would you feel? What might happen next? What resources could you call on? What new directions could you consider? What specifically makes this fear so powerful for you? Often, we refuse to look squarely at what frightens us most, and so the fear is magnified by a multiplicity of undefined consequences that in fact we could handle if we faced them.

BEHAVIORS AND CONSEQUENCES It's time to start challenging the beliefs that have robbed you of the life you deserve. I want you to take off the blinders you've been wearing so you can identify four prevalent negative behaviors in your life—denial, faulty initial assumptions, inertia, and deceptive masking (for a good working definition of behavior, see pages 14–17 in *Life Strategies*).

To begin, look back over the history of your life you just created. Find ten key events or outcomes in your life that you did not want or need, and record them below. After each event or outcome, list the choices you made that set you up for it.

For example, if your house was burglarized at Christmas-time while you attended an evening church service, you might justifiably feel violated. But you may have contributed to that victimization. Objectively analyzing that possibility is useful. Did you leave your house unlocked while you ran up to the church for a short period of time? Did you leave your windows open to display your Christmas tree, at the same time making it obvious that no one was home? Did you leave your garage door open, perhaps anticipating a delivery from a store? In other words, even though it was not your fault that you were burglarized, you may have some accountability because you made yourself an "easy mark." As you review the ten key events or outcomes in your life that you did not want or need, take a hard, uncensored look at how you contributed to making yourself vulnerable to the negative outcomes.

1 — EVENT:
  Choices:

2 — EVENT:
  Choices:

3 — **EVENT:**
Choices:

4 — **EVENT:**
Choices:

5 — **EVENT:**
Choices:

6 — **EVENT:**
Choices:

7 — **EVENT:**
Choices:

8 — **EVENT:**
Choices:

9 — EVENT:
  Choices:

10 — EVENT:
  Choices:

Now go back to the epidemic behaviors—denial, faulty initial assumptions, inertia, and deceptive masking. If you haven't already identified what roles these behaviors played in each of the events or outcomes above, do so now.

For the next step, you'll have to think in new ways. You'll have to question all your assumptions. Most importantly, you'll need to continue to look for *results or outcomes you did not want or need* that were created by these behaviors in your life.

1 — What are the five most important ways you lived in *denial?* What outcomes resulted?

2 — List the top five instances and their results when you based your choices on *faulty initial assumptions.*

3 — Describe five occasions when you were stuck in *inertia.*

4—What are five specific ways in which you hid behind your *deceptive mask*? What happened in your life as a result?

WHAT DO I WANT TO CHANGE?

Try answering these questions. Remember! This is your chance to get real! If you don't acknowledge what isn't working in your life, you can't create realistic goals and strategies to change it.

What do you hate about yourself?

Make a list, and be specific! For example: "I hate that I cave in every time someone disagrees with my opinion." "I hate that I eat even when I'm not hungry." "I hate the way I giggle when I'm nervous." "I hate the way I scream at the kids when I get upset."

What do you hate about your life?

Again, the more specific you are, the more helpful this list will be as you create your goals and strategies. You might say: "I hate the way my life partner orders me around." "I hate that my next-door neighbors play their stereo so loud and so late at night." "I hate the way my clothes look on me." "I hate how boring my job is."

WHAT DO I WANT?

So far, you've concentrated on where you are and where you've been. You've identified aspects of your history—personal, relational, professional, familial, and spiritual—that have had important effects on your present life. And you've pinpointed life circumstances that you want to eliminate, minimize, or manage better. Now it's time to get real about where you want to go from here. You'll be given a number of opportunities to re-evaluate the following questions and your answers to them. But right now, I want you to take an honest stab at stating what you would consider "success." What will you have to create in your life in order for you to say, "Bingo! That is *it!*"?

At this point, it's vital that you distinguish between what you really want in life ("it") and some of the things that only symbolize what you want. For example, you may want an important job, but if you dig more deeply and get more honest with yourself, you realize that the job itself is not really the point. You want the job because it will help you feel good about yourself and your ability to provide. So what you really want is self-esteem and a sense of security—the important job is only one of many potential sources for the experience you want. The following exercise takes you through a series of three questions in a repeating pattern: What do you want? What must you do to have it? How will you feel when you get it? As you answer each set of questions, you will begin to uncover the experience you are longing to achieve and to separate it from the things that only symbolize that experience to you. (For an example of this assignment in action, see pages 219–223 in *Life Strategies*.)

Round One   1—What do you want?

2—What must you do to get it?

3—How will you feel when you get it?

Round Two 1—So what you really want is . . . (Finish the sentence using your answer to the last question in Round One.)

2—What must you do to get it?

3—How will you feel when you get it?

Round Three 1—So what you really want is . . . (Finish the sentence using your answer to the last question in Round Two.)

2—What must you do to get it?

3—How will you feel when you get it?

WHAT'S
WORKING? Review your history once again, only this time find ten *positive* events or outcomes, and list them below. What choices did you make that contributed to each?

1—EVENT:
Choices:

2 — EVENT:

Choices:

3 — EVENT:

Choices:

4 — EVENT:

Choices:

5 — EVENT:

Choices:

6 — EVENT:

Choices:

7 — EVENT:

Choices:

8 — EVENT:

Choices:

9 — EVENT:
Choices:

10 — EVENT:
Choices:

Take a good long look at yourself. What do you see in the choices and outcomes above that you value or treasure about yourself? Find five "quality" words or phrases that describe what you appreciate most about you.

1.

2.

3.

4.

5.

The qualities you just identified are important resources in your life strategy. As important as it is to learn from your mistakes, you must also learn from your successes. If you can define the behaviors, choices, and beliefs that have led to success in your life, then you will know to add them as ingredients to your strategy as you face any present or future challenges. Learn from your successes. Emulate those times in your life when the outcome has been what you wanted.

EXCUSES I'LL TELL MYSELF

I want you to do one more little assignment before you move on to study the Life Laws and then create a personal life strategy. I want you to sit down and write "The Story I'll Tell Myself if I Don't Create Meaningful and Lasting Change After Reading and Studying *Life Strategies: Doing What Works, Doing What Matters.*" I want you to be creative, thorough, and brutally honest. You know your typical excuses, rationalizations, and justifications for failure. Figure out now which excuses you'll use in the event that you quit short of the goal this time. This is your chance to identify some of the key ways in which you've been sabotaging yourself. Write a minimum of one full page, including all of your excuses, whining, blaming, rationalizations, and so forth. Can you tell it like it is? Here you go.

"After reading and studying the book, I did not create meaningful and lasting change because . . ."

PART II

GET SMART

Learning the Ten Life Laws

Before you begin this portion of the *Life Strategies Workbook*, read chapters 2 through 11 on the ten Life Laws in *Life Strategies: Doing What Works, Doing What Matters.*

Knowledge is power. You only have to look around you at the "winners" to see that they're winning because they know what they need to know. This section of the *Life Strategies Workbook* is designed to give you the opportunity to learn the ten Life Laws on two levels: first, to understand how they are already at work—for better or worse—in your life; and second, to discover how you can make them *work for you* now and in the future.

Complete each of the following exercises thoroughly and honestly. Take the time to think in new and different ways as you work your way through the Life Laws. The goal is to figure out what isn't working in your life and make it work—but you can't *do* it until you *know* it!

LIFE LAW #1   *You Either Get It, or You Don't*

Your Strategy: Become one of those who get it. Break the code of human nature, and find out what makes people tick. Learn why you and other people do what they do, and don't do what they don't.

Life is not a mystery. The school of life is going on all around you. You need to be awake to the lessons life can teach you if you want to be one of the ones who "gets it." You need to tune in to how you and others behave and why. You need to understand the cause-and-effect relationships that grow out of your and others' behavior. Only then will you learn how to make things happen in the way you want.

It's time to start learning "the ropes" of your own life. As you work through the following exercises, continue to be ruthlessly honest with yourself. Pay attention to the attitudes you've brought with you so far. Be ready to question them in the light of this primary Life Law.

BLIND-FAITH PATTERNS

Keep your time line and life history handy for this exercise. You'll be identifying the patterns that, at some point in your life, you adopted on blind faith. Such patterns could be as simple as how to cook a pot roast or as complex as how to show someone you love them. You may have accepted the input from a parent, a friend, a teacher, or a spiritual counselor. The pattern may contain valuable truth, or it may be nothing more than somebody else's ignorance in action. The point is to disclose to yourself as many blind-faith patterns in your own life as you can. Once you've done that, you'll be able to test whether they are actually working for you or not. Be willing to challenge every belief in your life. There are no sacred cows. Do not feel guilty about challenging those things that you believe are "morally right." Any value that will not withstand challenge should not be embraced and maintained. If the belief is truly solid, it will withstand the challenge, and you can go forward with renewed conviction as to its appropriateness and healthfulness.

Begin with your personal life. What do you do on autopilot? Examine your daily schedule; eating and exercise habits; recreational choices; "down" time behavior; typical responses to stress; "half-full" or "half-empty" ways of viewing life; attitudes toward learning new ways of doing or seeing. For example, when someone offers advice, do you respond in the way one of your parents might have responded, perhaps with defensiveness and a negative judgment of the would-be advisor? In social situations, do you eat and drink far more than what is in keeping with your weight management goals because your family culture models that behavior? Do you typically drop in front of the television when pressing demands have been met without thinking either about what you might do instead or whether you're really gaining anything from what you're watching—because you've done it all your life? Pinpoint at least ten patterns of living that you have accepted without questioning them.

1.

2.

3.

4.

5.

6.

7.

8.

9.

10.

Look at your professional life. This includes whatever you do as your work, whether it's full-time homemaking, office work, teaching, construction, or anything else. Look at the way you plan your workday; how you relate to coworkers; what attitudes you have about the work, customers, workload, and boss. Pinpoint at least ten patterns that you've accepted without questioning or challenging them.

1.

2.

3.

4.

5.

6.

7.

8.

9.

10.

Examine your family life. Here, more than anywhere, you're likely to find hand-me-down patterns of behaviors and attitudes. You may not even like these attitudes or behaviors, but you hang on to them because you've never acknowledged them or created a strategy to change them. Go back to "My Family Legacy" on page 7 in Part I of this workbook. Review your answers and look for patterns in your parents and other significant family members that you've duplicated in your own life. List at least ten blind-faith patterns below.

1.

2.

3.

4.

5.

6.

7.

8.

9.

10.

Repeat the exercise with your social life in view. Consider how you treat friends, neighbors, other parents at school, fellow members of volunteer groups, and so on. Examine your "knee-jerk" reactions. Think about what typically makes you feel angry and how you handle it; what typically leads to behavior you later regret; what you expect from others; and what you tend to get from others. Remember that there are no accidents. There are specific causes for the effects you experience in your social life. Find and write down at least ten patterns in this part of your life that you've adopted without consciously choosing them.

1.

2.

3.

4.

5.

6.

7.

8.

9.

10.

DOING
SOMETHING
DIFFERENT
You don't have to live in your unquestioned patterns! You've just identified at least forty blind-faith patterns. Now I want you to exercise your choice muscles a little. The more you acknowledge and experiment with your ability to choose how you live,

the more satisfying, successful, and enjoyable your life will become. So start now. Shake it up! Here are a few suggestions for changing your day-to-day life, just to prove you can do it. Make a deal with yourself. Change one thing every day for the next two weeks. You can start with my suggestions, but add some of your own. Be creative. Be courageous. For example:

Rearrange your bedroom.
Reorganize your wardrobe, making some new combinations.
Unplug your television for a week to ten days (if the cord is removable, take it off and put it in the top of a closet).
Play music in your house in the mornings and early afternoons (or if you're a perennial music-player, try silence for a while).
Put clutter away every day.
Exercise on your way home instead of trying to do it at home.

Add some ideas of your own. Choose five additional changes and record them here.

1.

2.

3.

4.

5.

HUNTING FOR THE "GRAY DOGS"

We all know folks—the "Gray Dogs" of life (see page 43 of the book *Life Strategies*)—who have the experience and common-sense wisdom necessary to "break the code" in some area of our lives. They may work with us, live in our neighborhood, belong to our church or our family, or cut our hair.

Right now, identify three Gray Dogs in your life. List their names on page 35.

Commit yourself to observing each Gray Dog closely for the next two weeks. If you won't be seeing the Gray Dog, spend some time remembering the wisdom-in-action you've observed in the past.

After each of the names you listed below, prove that the person you've named is an authentic Gray Dog by describing two or three examples of his or her wisdom in action.

Finally, put words in the mouths of each of your Gray Dogs. Write one piece of *advice to yourself*, based on what you've observed about that person and what you now realize that you could learn from him or her. In other words, consider the area of your own life in which this person's wisdom is especially meaningful to you and write it out as personal advice: "My advice to you, [your name], is . . ." and finish the sentence.

NAME:
Examples:

Advice:

NAME:
Examples:

Advice:

NAME:
Examples:

Advice:

LEARNING TO KNOW OTHERS An important part of developing your skill as the manager of your own life is understanding the lives and actions of others. When you know what makes someone—or a group of some-ones—tick, you have a much clearer view of what you have to offer. The list of questions below provides an excellent starting place for building the observation skills you need in order to become a more effective student of human nature. Choose three people you feel you know very well. Complete the questionnaire for each person. Put a star next to each question that you can't answer fully until you pay closer attention.

Name: 1 — What does this person value most in their life (for example, ethics, money, success, strength, compassion)? List the top three things in order of their importance to him or her.

2 — What are this person's expectancies and beliefs about how life does and should work? Try to describe this in one or two sentences.

3 — What resistances or predispositions—fears, biases, prejudices—does this person have? Identify five specifics.

4 — What positions or approaches or philosophies (among your own, for example) is this person most likely to reject or accept? Choose two you believe he or she would reject. Choose two you believe he or she would accept.

5 — What does this person need to hear from another person to be assured that that person is fundamentally "okay" and to be trusted?

6 — What sorts of things does this person consider relevant? Name three.

7 — How does this person feel about him- or herself (physically, intellectually, spiritually, vocationally, socially)?

8 — What does this person want most in his or her life?

Try to choose at least one person among the three who you can ask to answer the questions above, either as an oral "quiz" or on a separate sheet of paper, *after* you've answered about the person. How accurately did you answer for him or her?

Now try answering the same questions *about yourself*.

Name: 1 — What do you value most in your life? List the top three things in order of importance *to you*.

2 — What are your expectancies and beliefs about how life does and should work?

3 — What resistances or predispositions—fears, biases, prejudices—do you have? Identify five specifics.

4 — What positions or approaches or philosophies are you most
likely to reject or accept? Choose two you would reject.
Choose two you would accept.

5 — What do you need to hear from a person to be assured that
that person is "okay" and to be trusted?

6 — Name three things you consider relevant.

7 — How do you feel about yourself (physically, intellectually,
spiritually, vocationally, socially)?

8 — What do you want most in your life?

OBSERVATION PRACTICE Now that you've tested your knowledge of a few of the people you're closest to, try developing your observation skills among a wider circle of people. On pages 49–50 of *Life Strategies: Doing What Works, Doing What Matters*, you'll find a list of the ten most significant common characteristics that motivate people.

Copy this list onto a three-by-five-inch card and carry it with you for a week. Pull it out when you're taking a coffee break, when you're waiting for the bus, or when you're waiting for the soup to boil. Review it until you can repeat the ten points in your own words. At the same time, use the list to aid you in paying closer attention to those around you.

Throughout the week, look for specific examples of each of the ten characteristics in the people around you. Note each specific case on the card after the characteristic. Don't bother with a lot of detail. Time, place, and person (in code, if you want) will do. Keep this up until you've recorded at least one example of each.

Finally, experiment. Choose three of the ten characteristics. Tomorrow, practice each of the three in a real-life interaction of your own. Then record the results below.

CHARACTERISTIC:
Outcome:

CHARACTERISTIC:
Outcome:

CHARACTERISTIC:
Outcome:

THE TURTLE SELF-TEST One of the most important people for you to observe and know inside-out is *you*. Most of us experience moments of "turtle behavior." When we're confronted with an opportunity to learn information that challenges what we think we know, we choose to pull back into our self-satisfied shells. Take the quiz below and see what your "turtle rating" is. Rate each statement from 1 to 5, according to how true it is of you (1 = almost never, 3 = sometimes, 5 = almost always).

_____ When someone contradicts me, my first reaction is to argue.

_____ I tend to make up my mind quickly.

_____ When someone asks me a question, I often sound more sure of the answer than I actually am.

_____ I'd rather win than be right.

_____ I know as much or more than most of the people I hang around with.

_____ Once I've made up my mind about something, I rarely change it.

_____ When I know I'm mistaken, I find it difficult to admit it.

_____ I spend as little time as possible with people who are smarter than me.

_____ I like talking better than listening.

_____ I consider my education complete.

Add up your score. If you rated 10 to 15, you're on the right track. Keep going. If you scored 16 to 35, you need to pay more attention to your "turtle" habits and find ways to change them. If you're in the 36 to 50 range, you're about to be inducted into the "Know-It-All Club" of boors and bullies. Time for some humility, soul-searching, and a major overhaul of your learning style. Become one of the ones who gets it!

LIFE LAW #2   *You Create Your Own Experience*

Your *Strategy:* Acknowledge and accept accountability for your life. Understand your role in creating the results that are in your life. Learn how to choose better so you have better.

You are about to find a variety of ways in which to answer the question, "How did I behave and choose my way to where I am?" Life Law #2 states unequivocally that you have been, are, and always will be accountable for your life—all of it. I'm not saying that every circumstance or event in your life is *your fault*. I am saying that you are accountable for how you respond. You are not a victim. The solutions to what's wrong with your life lie within you, the choices you make, and behaviors you choose now.

Remember, failing to accept this Life Law is a "deal-breaker." Only as you accept your own accountability for where you are and where you go next, only as you believe and understand that you create your own experience, will you be able to make an effective strategy to create the experience you want. You can't change the past, but you can sure change what you do with it.

OWNING MY FEELINGS

As you continue to study the ten Life Laws, you will come back to the question again and again, "What do I want to change?" Another way to ask the question is, "What is the life circumstance that I do not like?" Life Law #2 states that you are accountable for every circumstance you want to change. Accepting this Life Law makes it possible for you to accurately diagnose the problem and take charge of the solution. Start the process now by listing ten life circumstances that you do not like. Refer to "What Do I Want to Change?" on page 17 of this workbook to stimulate your thinking.

1.

2.

3.

4.

5.

6.

7.

8.

9.

10.

After you have listed ten life circumstances, use the space under each to identify how you feel about this circumstance. Use as specific a word as you can. If "anger" comes to mind, write it down, and then search for the emotion behind it (hurt, frustration, fear). If "sadness" occurs to you, look for the emotion that makes you sad (loneliness, regret, guilt). The point is to be as clear and accurate as possible about how you really feel, because the closer you get to the deepest emotion, the closer you'll get to the part you played in arriving where you are now.

Of the ten circumstances you just listed, put a star next

to the five that you most want to change. Finally, put the top five in order of importance to you, with the first being most urgent, and so forth. Now you're ready to start taking your accountability seriously.

WHAT DID I DO? Below, copy the life circumstance that you made number one on your list from the previous page. Then go on to take the test below. The checklist isn't meant to limit the possibilities. Use the extra space for additional choices and behaviors that you made that have landed you in this undesirable life circumstance.

Life Circumstance: What did I do to arrange the situation so that it happened in the way that it happened?

What did I do to make the result possible?

_____ Did I trust foolishly?

_____ Did I miss important warning signs?

_____ Did I fail to be clear about what I wanted?

_____ Did I con myself because I wanted it to be true?

What choices did I make that directly led to the result I did not want?

_____ Did I choose the wrong person or the wrong place?

_____ Did I choose what I chose for the wrong reasons?

_____ Did I choose the wrong time?

What did I *fail* to do that directly created the result I did not want?

_____ Did I fail to take needed action? If so, what was it?

_____ Did I fail to stand up for myself and claim my rights?

_____ Did I fail to ask for what I wanted?

_____ Did I fail to require enough of myself?

_____ Did I fail to tell somebody to go jump in the lake?

_____ Did I fail to treat myself with dignity and respect?

What actions do I now need to take in order to change?

_____ Do I need to start certain new behaviors? If so, what behaviors?

_____ Do I need to stop certain old behaviors? If so, what behaviors?

Where Was *I* When That Happened?

You've just identified some life circumstances in the present that you don't like. By completing the previous exercises, you've started the process of diagnosing your own accountability for it. Now try it from another angle. Reevaluate the history that may have previously had you cast, at least in your mind, as a victim. Using the personal history and time line you created in Part I, think back through the various stages of your life, and identify the five most significant times in your life when, before now, you felt that you had been victimized, mistreated, or in some way unfairly dealt with. Describe these situations with enough detail that you can capture the emotion of each. Leave some space under each of the five situations to write some other things.

1.

2.

3.

4.

5.

Now go back to each description. Beneath it, identify how you were in fact accountable for your bad result. Use the questions and checklists in the previous exercise to guide you as you rethink the victim version of your history. You are not allowed to blame anyone else here! Put aside what "they" did. This is about what *you* did or didn't do, what *you* chose, and how *you* turned a blind eye to important warning signs. This is not busy work, so don't treat it as such. This is the beginning of a new way of thinking and a better way of living.

ERASING THE NEGATIVE "TAPES"

One of the ways you can learn to make accountability a way of life is to get rid of the self-defeating, negative conversations you hold with and about yourself every day. Such conversations—negative "tapes"—that you play over and over in your thoughts have the power to keep you from making different choices or developing new behaviors. On page 70 of *Life Strategies: Doing What Works, Doing What Matters,* you'll find a list of twelve typical negative statements. Use these to help you identify the negative tapes you're running in your own head. Make a list below of your top ten negative tapes.

1.

2.

3.

4.

5.

6.

7.

8.

9.

10.

Now transfer the list, in shortened form if need be, to an index card that you can carry with you. Any time you hear yourself running another negative tape, write it on the card. Check yourself to see how often you're running the tapes throughout your day.

EVALUATING MY STYLE

It's vital to understand the part you are playing in the way that others treat you and respond to you. Until you reckon with the principle of reciprocity in your experience with others, you'll lack a necessary tool to making your life what you want it to be. Begin by observing the styles of the people around you. Review, on pages 73–80 of *Life Strategies*, the descriptions of each of the styles that follow here. Find *at least* one person who fits each description, and record his or her name or initials next to the style. Then describe for yourself a situation in which you saw one of these people in action and the result in the way others treated him or her.

_____ The Porcupine _____ Drama Queen

_____ Paws Up _____ Victim

_____ King or Queen of _____ Einstein Analyzer
the Forest _____ Conspirator Gossip

_____ The Poser _____ Yeah, But

_____ People-Eater _____ Scarlett O'Hara

_____ The Mask _____ Chicken Little
_____ Jekyll-and-Hyde _____ Whiner
_____ Goody Two-Shoes _____ Guiltmonger
_____ Perfecto

Now go back and put a check mark in the space before every style that describes you. In the space below, write your own one-paragraph description of your overall style.

List five ways in which you can see your style causing negative responses from others. Specifically, identify a time and circumstance with a specific individual when you have exhibited one of your "stylistic anomalies" and elicited a negative reaction such as withdrawal, rejection, criticism, or some other reaction you did not want. By being specific, you force yourself to move from theory to fact regarding how you are creating your own experience.

1.

2.

3.

4.

5.

What positive style traits can you see? How do people typically respond to each?

AM I READY?   Before you go on to Life Law #3, look back over the work you have done. Review the ways that your life has been less than you want it to be and how you have chosen to get there. Then answer the true-false statements below.

	True	False
I am accountable for all of my life.	____	____
It is not too late to change the way I think, choose, and behave.	____	____
I deserve so much more than the life I have now.	____	____
I will deny myself and the life I want no longer.	____	____

If you answered "true" to all of the above, you are ready to move on. If you answered "false" to one or more of the statements, you need to go back and reread Chapter 3 of *Life Strategies: Doing What Works, Doing What Matters*. Then review all of the work you have done on Life Law #2 in this workbook. Only when you can say *true!* to the four statements above will you be ready to take on this life-changing challenge.

LIFE LAW #3   *People Do What Works*

Your *Strategy:* Identify the payoffs that drive your behavior and that of others. Control the payoffs to control your life.

Underlying Life Law #3 is the immutable fact that no one, including you, continues to do something that gives him or her only negative, unwanted results. If you continue to behave in a certain way, or to make a certain set of choices, you do so because at some level, whether you realize it or not, you are getting results you want. They may not be healthy results, but at some level you must want them, and so you continue to do what gives them to you.

Changing behaviors or choices that bring about results that run counter to the life changes you most want may present your greatest challenge when you begin to make your life plan. It is critically important that you uncover the payoffs that lead you to counterproductive or self-destructive choices. Only then will you be equipped to successfully make the changes you most want to make. The following exercises will help you find out what causes you to do what you hate despite the pain it produces. Be real. Be honest. You may find it helpful to reread the examples I have included on pages 93–94 in *Life Strategies*. Be ready to add a vital piece of human knowledge to what you've learned so far.

How often have you started a new year, or a new job, or a new relationship, with an enthusiastic promise to yourself that you'll finally get rid of that behavior that has plagued you and your best intentions in the past? Check off any of the following statements that describe you. Then, in the space provided, write out five more statements that describe what you're currently doing in your life that, *based on results,* is not working.

_____ I eat when I'm not hungry or when I don't want to eat.

_____ I smoke when I don't want to smoke.

_____ I lose my temper and argue in front of the kids (or others who I'd rather did not see it).

_____ I give in to the demands of others when it is the last thing I want to do.

_____ I choke under pressure when I'm aiming for peak performance.

_____ I feel guilty when I wish I didn't, so that I make decisions that are self-destructive.

_____ I spend a huge amount of time doing activities I don't really want to do.

_____ I "veg" out in front of the television when I'd rather read, exercise, or spend time with my family or friends.

_____ I regularly procrastinate, putting off the activities or projects that matter most to me.

_____ I cheat on someone whom I really want to honor with faithfulness and honesty.

_____ I spend more money than I can afford even though I want to get my finances under control.

1.

2.

3.

4.

5.

Now you've identified some specific choices that you continue to make even though you know that they keep you from what you want. Put a bookmark on this page. You'll come back to it many times.

THE
"CURRENCY"
OF LIFE

The list below names the most important categories of life "income." Virtually every payoff in your life will fall under one of these. Read through the list carefully, and if you don't understand any of the categories, reread pages 95–98 in *Life Strategies* to bring yourself up to speed. I want you to consider the relative importance of each of these larger categories in your life. Only as you become familiar with thinking about them will you be able to develop the habit of identifying them when you choose or behave in counterproductive ways. Begin by giving each of the following incomes a rating of 1 to 5, according to how important you consider it to be in your life (make 1 the highest value and 5 the lowest).

Monetary   _____
Psychological   _____
Spiritual   _____
Physical   _____
Achievement   _____
Social   _____

Now go through the list again, this time writing next to each category the particular forms that specific currency takes in your life. Reread the specifics I've listed in the *Life Strategies* book to identify any that ring true for you.

WHAT NEEDS TO CHANGE?

Let's take the discussion of Life Law #3 to a deeper level and deal with the details of your life. In the space below, write a list of the five most frustrating and persistent negative behavioral patterns or situations in your life.

Identify the specific behavior.
Describe the pattern.
Put into words the degree of its intensity.
Write two or three sentences explaining why you find this behavior or situation negative.

Make your best effort to analyze, identify, and write down the payoff that is feeding and maintaining this negative behavioral pattern. The more thorough and honest you are, the more helpful this exercise will be.

BEHAVIOR #1:

BEHAVIOR #2:

BEHAVIOR #3:

BEHAVIOR #4:

BEHAVIOR #5:

If you're having difficulty identifying payoffs, go back and review the categories and subcategories you've already worked on in "The 'Currency' of Life" exercise on page 55. Then ask yourself the following:

1—What do I gain through this behavior?

2—What do I avoid?

3—How does this behavior serve my need to feel accepted, safe, or in control?

4—What risks does it allow me to sideline?

5—What specific pain am I able to deflect through this behavior?

6—What immediate gratification am I trading for what deferred gratification?

7—Is there a payoff for me because others observe this behavior? If so, what is it?

8—Does it make my life easier (although not better)? In what way?

Throughout this analysis, keep in mind that gains and avoidances can come from any one or more of the life currencies. For each behavior, run down the list of currencies: monetary, psychological, physical, spiritual, achievement, and social.

MY SUCCESS STORIES — Let's turn the tables now. Payoffs are as significant as motivators in what works in your life as they are in what doesn't work. What are the five smartest things you've ever done? (For example, "I went to night school to finish my degree." "I chose the lower-paying position so I could be home with children after school." "I called off the wedding even though the invitations had already gone out.") Why did each work? Specifically, what did you get out of each? (For instance, self-esteem, a better relationship, freedom to choose better.) If you stopped doing what was working, *why* did you stop? ("I was afraid I would fail." "I got lazy." "I accepted bad advice instead of thinking for myself.")

1.
Payoff:

2.
Payoff:

3.
Payoff:

4.
Payoff:

5.
Payoff:

THE "CURRENCY" EXCHANGE

You've identified several negative behaviors and dug deep to discover the payoffs that keep you from changing them. You've also looked at some of the payoffs that motivated positive, successful behaviors. Put all this investigation to good use. In the space below, copy the list of five behaviors or situations that you identified in "What Needs to Change?" on page 56. After each one, describe how you would like it to change. Then carefully consider what payoff or payoffs the change could offer. Write these below the specific change.

BEHAVIOR OR SITUATION:
Needed change:
Potential payoff(s):

BEHAVIOR OR SITUATION:
Needed change:
Potential payoff(s):

BEHAVIOR OR SITUATION:
Needed change:
Potential payoff(s):

BEHAVIOR OR SITUATION:
Needed change:
Potential payoff(s):

BEHAVIOR OR SITUATION:
Needed change:
Potential payoff(s):

ASSESSING MY RISK AVERSION

People resist change. Whether for reasons of laziness, fear, losing a sense of control, or something else, we all act like a "body at rest" sometimes. If we're at rest, we tend to stay at rest. The sort of diagnosis you've been doing here is likely to feel risky, even while it may make you feel excited. As a result, the level of your risk aversion could very well short-circuit the potential of finally making the life changes you need and want.

Ask yourself now, "Am I addicted, invisibly, to the sense of security that comes from avoiding pain and risk?" Be ruthless in your honesty. Think about the five behaviors or situations you've been examining in this section. Is the fear of risk one major reason that you've stranded yourself in these negative patterns?

Of the five negative situations or behaviors you described, choose the one that troubles you most. In the space below, imagine yourself living out the change you've described. Write a story describing the risks you must face to get there. Which is scariest to you? Why? What would you risk losing? Is it worth hanging on to? Are you worth the risks?

LIFE LAW #4   *You Can't Change What You Don't Acknowledge*

Your *Strategy:* Get real with yourself about your life and everybody in it. Be truthful about what isn't working in your life. Stop making excuses and start making results.

Have you ever told a "little white lie"? If you're like the rest of the human race, you've told more than one. Some of the time, the person you lied to was you. And some of the time, the lie was not a "little white" one. Life Law #4 zeroes in on the destructive pattern of denial—the web of lies we tell ourselves rather than face the painful truth. Without a solid understanding of this law and how it applies specifically to you, no amount of intention or hard work will take you where you want to go. Until you figure out where you are, you won't be able to set your course for where you *want* to be. Unless you own up to the ways in which you've been dishonest with yourself, you'll be looking in the wrong places for answers.

I want you to get real and acknowledge the lies you've been telling yourself. Use the exercises that follow to honestly face yourself, your circumstances, and your relationships. Look head-on at your life as it really is so you can shed the burdens that are holding you down.

THE FIB HABIT Don't believe you have a dishonest bone in your body? For the next three days, keep a note card in your pocket. Every time you say something that is not 100 percent true, take note and remember to write it down as soon as you can. Do the same every time you *imply* something that is not true. Do it every time you simply *omit* the truth, as well. After the three days, transfer everything you've written from the note card to the space below, leaving some writing space after each.

Life Law #4 states that you can't change what you don't acknowledge. As you do this exercise, acknowledge that you're just as prone to the habit of dishonesty as the next person. When you begin to recognize the many small ways every day that you skirt the truth, you'll gain the valuable skill of testing the truth in the larger patterns of your life. This is all about learning to recognize, admit, and change the pattern of dishonesty.

Once you've transferred your list of lies, assess each one and answer these questions.

Why did I fail to tell the truth?
What was my payoff for lying?
What was I afraid of losing if I told the truth?

Choose one situation from your list and rewrite it in the space below. Describe what would have happened if you'd chosen to be truthful instead. How would the situation have been different? How would the other person or people present have reacted? How would you have felt while you were speaking the truth? How would you have felt afterward?

What positive payoffs can you imagine from telling the truth in this situation?

Repeat this experiment with several more of the lies above.

TWENTY THINGS I HATE TO ADMIT

You've just conducted an observation exercise about your honesty habits in relation to others. Many of the same reasons for why you choose to lie to others underlie your decision to lie to yourself. Right now, make a list of the twenty things you most hate to admit to yourself. To get started, think about specific areas in your life in which you feel the need to be right. What truth about you, your life, your situation, or a relationship do you have to deny in order to be right? What do you need to cover up in order to feel comfortable?

1.

2.

3.

4.

5.

6.

7.

8.

9.

10.

11.

12.

13.

14.

15.

16.

17.

18.

19.

20.

NO EXCUSES   The list you created in the previous exercise gives you details of some specific ways in which you practice dishonesty with yourself. Those twenty specifics fall into larger categories. When you can see and acknowledge the larger patterns, you'll be able to identify other specific ways in which you're avoiding the truth, making positive change impossible.

Below you'll find several hard questions you need to ask yourself if you're going to be honest enough to set and reach important goals for change later in the workbook.

Begin by reading through the list of questions. Note the ones to which you answered "yes." Then refer back to your list of twenty items in the last exercise. For every "yes" answer on this page, find each item in the list that is a specific example of why you continue to follow these negative patterns. Check off the items on your list as you go.

Next, look at any items that you didn't check off. For each, write your own "hard question" to describe the way you've been lying to yourself in that specific case.

1 — Am I living like a loser?

2 — Am I lazy? Am I simply not requiring enough of myself?

3 — Is my life a dead-end journey, heading nowhere?

4 — Am I scared? Am I playing this game with sweaty palms?

5 — Is my marriage (or significant relationship) in the ditch and emotionally defunct?

6 — Are my kids living like losers and self-destructing in their own right?

7 — Do I have no goals? Am I just going through the motions, day after day?

8 — Am I continually making promises to myself that I never, ever keep?

9 — (Write your own question.)

10 — (Write your own question.)

RATING MY REALISM

You're in the process of doing what matters so you can start living a life that works for you. No matter what's going on, no matter what's going wrong, your life is not too bad to fix, if you're willing to face what needs fixing. You've identified some specific ways in which you're living in denial. You've looked at the "how." Now continue to look for the "why." The self-assessment test below can help you figure out whether you have unrealistic expectations about yourself, your life, and your relationships. If you do, you're setting yourself up for denial. The gap between your pie-in-the-sky expectations and real life makes honesty just too painful.

Give yourself a rating of 1 to 5 for each statement (1 = almost never, 3 = sometimes, 5 = almost always). Before you rate each one, think of *specific instances* in your life and *be brutally honest.*

_____ I expect love to conquer all in a romantic relationship.

_____ I demand perfection of my personal behavior.

_____ I am let down when the first excitement of a new situation or relationship wears off.

_____ I tend to "wait and see" when something seems to be going wrong.

_____ I choose to hear good news before bad news.

_____ I try to maintain the appearance of happiness and well-being in front of neighbors, church friends, extended family, work colleagues, and others.

_____ I look for the best and make excuses for the worst in those around me.

_____ I tend to procrastinate when facing a job or decision that is painful or unpleasant to me.

_____ I avoid news stories that are upsetting to me.

_____ I am taken by surprise when others don't like me or object to the way I behave.

Now add up the points in the left column. If you scored 10 to 15, you're either still lying big-time to yourself and need to start all over, or you live with a relatively realistic perspective that you can strengthen and build on as you continue through the Life Laws.

A score of 21 to 34 indicates that there are areas of your life in which you're fooling yourself. Pay close attention to any statement above that you gave a rating higher than 2, and acknowledge the specific problems each reveals.

A score of 35 to 50 means you're living in a dreamworld most of the time. Get serious about acknowledging how much you're allowing gullibility and naïveté to keep you from success. This is the crucial first step to changing.

GETTING
WHAT I
DON'T WANT

If you've become serious about facing yourself in this section, you've seen that you are not perfect and that you are living with your share of accumulated baggage. You need to give yourself permission to be the person you are with the distorted thoughts, feelings, and reactions that are a part of you right now.

As one of two final exercises in acknowledging what you want and need to change to have a successful life, take another look at the events in your life that have changed you dramatically. Choose what you consider to be the five most influential events. Maybe one is a lost love or the death of a loved one. Maybe one is a disastrous marriage or the failure of nerve at a critical moment. Maybe you've been cheated on or been falsely accused or violated in some way. Whatever they are, choose the top five events, and write them below. But don't stop there.

Next, ask yourself, "How does this make me feel *now?*" If you're bitter, scared, or lonely, say so. If you're angry, admit it. If you feel like a louse or a loser, write it down. Unless you acknowledge the characteristics in you that have grown from your experiences, you'll never be able to leave those experiences behind. You have to face them to replace them.

WHAT HAPPENED:
How I feel now:

WHAT HAPPENED:
How I feel now:

WHAT HAPPENED:
How I feel now:

WHAT HAPPENED:
How I feel now:

WHAT HAPPENED:
How I feel now:

THE HAPPIEST TIME IN MY LIFE

You're doing the hard work of diagnosing where you are so you can move ahead. The distortions you identified in the last exercise are only part of the picture. Now look at another part. Describe below the happiest time in your life, whenever that was. Maybe you were six years old at the time, or maybe it just occurred two weeks ago.

Describe yourself in as much detail as you can. How old are you? Where do you live? Describe how you look. What do you usually wear at this point in your life? Who are you spending time with? What matters to you? What are you proud of? How much money do you have? What do you do for fun? How do you spend a typical day? Where do you look for your security? How do you feel? Are you peaceful? Proud? Secure? Do you feel like you belong, like you are valued or respected? Describe your sense of the part you play in the world around you. What is it about this time that makes it the happiest?

Now describe what happened. If you had a happiest time in the past, it had a beginning and an end. What happened to end it? Did you change? Did the world change? Did someone do something to you? Recognize that something or some series of things occurred to end the happiest time of your life. Perhaps your innocence died or some intense experience changed the way you viewed reality. Identify the specifics that changed to end the happiest time. Be as complete and careful in your description as you can, including all the details you can recall. Name cause and responsibility as fully as possible.

What would it take for you to return to that life experience of happiness now? Answer as fully and completely as you are able, taking full responsibility for creating your own experience in this life.

LIFE LAW #5 *Life Rewards Action*

Your Strategy: Make careful decisions and then pull the trigger. Learn that the world couldn't care less about thoughts without actions.

You've come this far, and you've done a lot of honest assessing. You don't like where you are in your life, and you've been getting in touch with what you don't like, why you're there, and how you'd like to change. But this is not a book about good intentions and great insights. This is a book that is geared to transforming your understanding into planning and action.

Right now, I want you to put all your excuses on hold. I want you to commit to measuring your life and its quality based on results, not on what you want, hope for, or intend. You can change. You can get rid of your typical behaviors and your list of reasons why you *don't* change, and begin to act. The exercises that follow will help you translate hopes and intentions into actions. Nobody cares about your good intentions. They care about what you do.

THE RUT TEST   Start by finding out what sort of stimuli you provide to the world. The questions you need to answer here are, "Have my behaviors landed me in a rut of inertia? Have I stopped taking the kinds of actions that create quality results, and instead settled into a hum-drum, going-through-the-motions lifestyle?" The Rut Test will let you see how you measure up on the action/inertia scale. Remember Life Law #4: *You Can't Change What You Don't Acknowledge.* Circle *admit* or *deny* in response to each of the questions, based on how you really are living. No more lies, just the truth.

1 — Do you spend a high percentage of your free time as a "couch potato," watching ridiculous sitcoms or "blood and guts" dramas on television?   **Admit Deny**

2 — When you're at home, do you put on the same house dress, T-shirt and baggy shorts, or pajamas so often it's regarded as your "uniform"?   **Admit Deny**

3 — Do you stand at the refrigerator, staring into it, as if you really might discover something that wasn't there when you looked five minutes ago?   **Admit Deny**

4 — Do you treat life as though it is a spectator sport, and you are in the cheap seats?   **Admit Deny**

5 — Do you actually live vicariously through characters on TV, and discuss them as though they are real people?   **Admit Deny**

6 — Do you actually count and recount the items in your grocery cart before you venture into the express line?   **Admit Deny**

7 — Is your job or your kids all you ever talk about?   **Admit Deny**

8 — On the rare occasions you decide to go out, do you spend thirty minutes debating where to go? **Admit Deny**

9 — Do you only eat out at places where you have to look up rather than down at the menu? **Admit Deny**

10 — Do you have sex quarterly, and in less than four minutes, so you can time it with commercial breaks? **Admit Deny**

11 — Do you fantasize about things you never actually do? **Admit Deny**

12 — Are you suspicious of people who look really happy, because it just doesn't seem possible? **Admit Deny**

13 — Do you have a lesser standard of conduct when you are alone than when you are with others? **Admit Deny**

14 — Is the most exciting thing that's ever likely to occur in your life something that has already happened? **Admit Deny**

15 — When you awaken, do you dread starting another day? **Admit Deny**

16 — Do you feel alone, even when people are around? **Admit Deny**

17 — Do your appearance and your standards of personal grooming seem to be on the decline? **Admit Deny**

18 — Is your goal in life simply to get by for another week or month? **Admit Deny**

19 — Do you say "no" a really high percentage of the time, no matter what the question is? **Admit Deny**

20 — In order for you to meet someone new, would they have to throw themselves on the hood of your car, or pull a chair up in front of your TV set? **Admit Deny**

If you answered "admit" to eight or more of these items, you're in a rut. If you answered "admit" to twelve or more, we'd better send out a search party. No matter what your score, if your life is more talk than action, it's time to start measuring your own life by the standard the world uses—results!

LOST INTENTIONS

Inertia is one of those weeds in life that multiplies if you don't get rid of it. The less you do, the less you tend or want to do, and before you know it, you're sitting in the bleachers watching other folks win the game.

Look back over the life story you wrote in Part I of this workbook. As you review your past, pick out five *important* intentions you had that you failed to fulfill with action. For example, maybe you meant to pay a visit to your favorite grandparent when he or she was ailing, but you waited too long and the grandparent died. Or you designated a specific month to lose the extra five pounds you just gained, but instead went on gaining. Or you promised yourself you would send your book manuscript to a publisher, but chickened out, and the manuscript was thrown out by accident in a move. Record your own lost intentions in the spaces provided below. Then imagine what would have happened if you had followed through instead of letting yourself down (you told your grandparent all that he or she meant to you before you lost that dear one; you lost the extra weight before it became an overwhelming prospect and remained trim; you sent the book off and three publishers said "no," but the fourth loved it and made it a book). What could you have done differently that would have pushed you into the action you intended? What are some of the positive outcomes that could have resulted if you'd acted, in addition to the obvious ones? For instance, how would your feelings about yourself be different (proud, satisfied, focused, accomplished, without regrets)? What other actions might have followed the fulfilled intention (you became better at communicating your love to others, you took up a new recreational sport that added health and fun to your life, you had a more satisfying hobby or career that gave you great self-respect)?

INTENTION:

Different ways you could have handled yourself:

Potential outcome(s) if you had:

INTENTION:

Different ways you could have handled yourself:

Potential outcome(s) if you had:

INTENTION:

Different ways you could have handled yourself:

Potential outcome(s) if you had:

INTENTION:

Different ways you could have handled yourself:

Potential outcome(s) if you had:

INTENTION:

Different ways you could have handled yourself:

Potential outcome(s) if you had:

CATCHING UP WITH THE ONES I LOVE

If you're like most people, your good intentions include making time for people who are very important to you. One of the actions you need to take involves "catching up" emotionally with someone you love. We find it painful to acknowledge that we don't know how long we or those we love will survive in this life, and so we live in denial. We act as though we have all the time in the world. Well, guess what? We don't! You have no idea if that precious person will make it through today. Wouldn't it be tragic if you—or they—ran out of time before you overcame the inertia in your life and said what you have in your heart?

The issue of intended but unexpressed feelings is too important to put on hold for another moment. Make a list, right now, of the five to ten most important people in your life. Now, honestly—and from the heart—write down for each person everything that would be left unsaid if one or the other of you were to die at this very moment. Don't make the mistake of assuming people know. Even if they do, don't they deserve to hear it again? And wouldn't you live with regrets for the rest of your life if they died today and you hadn't spoken what's in your heart?

1.

2.

3.

4.

5.

6.

7.

8.

9.

10.

What practical means can you use to express what you've written here? *Right now,* choose one of the people above and take action. Write a letter, pick up the phone, log on to e-mail, or make a date to see the person and speak face-to-face. After you've taken action, choose another person on the list and do the same. Keep going until you've used up the whole list. Then think about whether the list should have included some other people. If so, make another list to act on. This is the difference between good intentions and creating your own experience.

THIS CALLS FOR ACTION! I hope that remembering the people you love and taking the action of expressing all that you love about them has made the rut you live in less appealing. Now let's put some more verbs in your sentences and some more action in your life.

The following chart has been divided into the five major life categories. Every one of these categories requires and deserves purposeful, meaningful, constructive actions. You'll be developing a specific personal life strategy later in this workbook, so the evaluation you do now will serve an extremely useful purpose as you go forward.

In each column, list the top four or five actions that you feel you need to take in that category. For example, the first row might read this way.

> **PERSONAL:** I need to take one day a week for rest and recreation.
>
> **RELATIONAL:** I need to take the initiative to clear up that misunderstanding with my sister once and for all.
>
> **PROFESSIONAL:** I need to put my job search first in order of importance right now.
>
> **FAMILIAL:** I need to establish a regular family conference time when everyone can have his or her say, and we can learn to work together better.
>
> **SPIRITUAL:** I need to establish a daily time of just ten minutes for reflection and prayer.

Don't get hung up here on details or immediate action. This is only a start, meant to identify some key areas of your life where action is needed. We'll get back to them later.

	Personal	Relational	Professional	Familial	Spiritual
1.					
2					
3.					
4.					
5.					

THIRTY TIMES I FAILED TO FOLLOW THROUGH

It's great to put what needs to be done in writing, as you've just done. It will be greater when you put it into action. But in the meantime, if you want your life to be different in the future from what it was in the past, you need to take an honest look at what has typically kept you from action.

Do it now. List thirty things that you've quit or failed to act on in this life—a relationship that you started with a person that you betrayed by cheating on him or her; a commitment to serve on a committee or do a volunteer job that you failed to follow through on; or a home repair project that you just failed to finish. After you've written them down, write down the reasons for your quitting. Did you want to avoid the pressure, the hard work, or the anxiety? Were you afraid that you would be rejected, that you would fail, or that you would lose something important to you? Did you think that you couldn't do it, or that you lacked the resources, or that someone was going to stop you? Be as specific as you can. Try to recall the actual feelings that were involved with your quitting. If you were just lazy, say so. If you became bored, write that. If you got cold feet, or feared you would be exposed as less than adequate for the job, or discovered that you didn't have the know-how or tools for the job, explore that here. You need to dig until you get to the bottom of your quitting.

1.
Why?

2.
Why?

3.
Why?

4.
Why?

5.
Why?

6.
Why?

7.
Why?

8.
Why?

9.
Why?

10.

Why?

11.

Why?

12.

Why?

13.

Why?

14.

Why?

15.

Why?

16.
Why?

17.
Why?

18.
Why?

19.
Why?

20.
Why?

21.
Why?

22.

Why?

23.

Why?

24.

Why?

25.

Why?

26.

Why?

27.

Why?

28.

Why?

29.

Why?

30.

Why?

My Top Twenty Achievements

Sometimes you haven't quit. You haven't climbed into the bleachers. You've played the game and won. You can learn as much or more from your own successes as you can from your failures. In the spaces below, list your best twenty achievements in your life so far. Don't tell me they don't exist, because I don't believe it. What are you proud of? Repairing a hurting marriage? Raising children who are people of character as adults? Making it possible for someone else to achieve a major success? Creating a home that is essentially loving and hospitable? Whatever it is, write it down here. After each achievement, remember what it took to act, and write that down, too. Then describe how you felt when you had taken the action needed to make it happen. As you remember and record these achievements, take note of the feelings, disciplines, and actions that gave you success. These are the elements in yourself and your world that you should be using to develop positive momentum in your life.

1.

2.

3.

4.

5.

6.

7.

8.

9.

10.

11.

12.

13.

14.

15.

16.

17.

18.

19.

20.

How do you feel looking back over what you have achieved so far?

TALKING
TO MYSELF

Sometimes incorporating Life Law #5—*Life Rewards Action*—requires that you take a risk. You have to step outside the comfort zone and challenge your natural desire to feel safe and secure. Resolve now to take the risks, to put in the effort, and to persist toward your goals. Don't quit this time. You may have to have a regular heart-to-heart with yourself to change your habit of inertia. That's fine, and here's an opportunity to practice. Below you'll find a list of assertions you may find yourself making when you're tempted to become inert. Read each assertion, then respond positively to it using Life Law #5 as your guide (see page 148 of *Life Strategies* for examples of how to do this).

"There will be setbacks."

"I may not succeed."

"People will reject me."

"I'll be a failure."

"Am I really worth it and capable of it?"

Have that heart-to-heart with yourself as often as you need to have it. Repeat the truth that life rewards action to yourself. And move ahead with the determination to take *action* and insist on *results*.

LIFE LAW #6   *There Is No Reality; Only Perception*

Y*our Strategy:* Identify the filters through which you view the world. Acknowledge your history without being controlled by it.

Life Law #2 states that you are accountable for how you respond to everything in your life. Your response creates your experience. But behind every response is a perception—the way you interpret or assign meaning to what you are experiencing.

Life Law #6 emphasizes the fact that the only reality you experience is a filtered one. You "see" through your personality, attitudes, and points of view. And you respond in your own unique style. I hope it's obvious by now that if you're ever going to "get it," if you're ever going to create the experience you want, you have to know what filters have defined your perception of reality up to now. You must become aware of the filters that have been placed over your eyes and mind throughout your learning history. Only then can you make constructive allowances for them. As Life Law #4 reveals, *You Can't Change What You Don't Acknowledge.*

By now, you've done a lot of looking back over your personal history. I want you to put that work to good use now.

The following exercises can help you discover what filters have distorted your outlook and find ways to create fresh, new perceptions that "rise above your raising."

THE PERCEPTION SELF-TEST

If you're going to identify your filters, you'll first have to acknowledge how your point of view affects your perception of reality. Begin by listing below ten specific instances when you reacted negatively—for example, to a first meeting with someone (when you thought someone talked down to you); to a conversation (in which you felt criticized); to a specific event (at which you were self-conscious); to an encounter in a public place (when you felt someone was rude); to a poor test score or evaluation (when you thought the teacher had a grudge); to the election of class officers or prom king and queen when you were in high school (and you decided the election was unfair); and so forth.

These are only examples. You need to remember your own negative responses and consider the possibility that your "reality" did not match objective reality because you experienced the event through a particular, negative filter of your own. After each instance, describe at least two alternative, positive ways in which you could have interpreted the person, encounter, or event. You need to understand that these alternative views may have as much or more validity as the view you took. For instance, many people who are terribly shy give others the impression that they are snobs. If you experience an encounter with such a person through a filter of poor self-esteem, you could easily read that shyness as a personal snub. A positive view might allow you to discover the shyness and get beyond it to a valuable relationship.

1.

Alternative interpretations:

2.

Alternative interpretations:

3.

Alternative Interpretations:

4.

Alternative interpretations:

5.

Alternative interpretations:

6.

Alternative interpretations:

7.

Alternative interpretations:

8.

Alternative interpretations:

9.

Alternative interpretations:

10.

Alternative interpretations:

SHAKING LOOSE MY FIXED BELIEFS

Your perspective grows in part out of life decisions you've made—those beliefs that you hold to be true. When a negative belief becomes fixed, or unaffected by new information, in your perceptual system, you're swimming in dangerous waters. Instead of responding to someone or something in a realistic, proactive way, you react in self-defeating ways on the basis of faulty initial assumptions: "He always puts himself first." "She never listens." "They just want another warm body to boost their numbers."

Test the presence of fixed beliefs in your own perceptual system. In the last exercise, you observed the effect of your point of view on the meaning you took from events and situations in your life. Look back over the list of ten negative perceptions from the last exercise. For each of the ten situations you described, use the space provided below to answer these two questions:

> What in my prior experience contributed to my negative perception in this specific instance?
> Did my response in this case reveal a fixed belief that is affecting my perception in other situations, as well? If so, what is it?

1.

2.

3.

4.

5.

6.

7.

8.

9.

10.

Rooting Out My Limiting Beliefs

Some of the most destructive fixed beliefs you hold are the ones that apply to yourself. A "limiting belief" is some negative self-perception that you've decided is true and accurate about you. I want you to challenge every single limiting belief you carry with you from day to day. Search your mind and heart for these limiting beliefs. It's the only way you'll be able to recognize them when they rear up to sabotage you, and the only way you'll be able to combat them.

To begin, here is a checklist of some limiting beliefs that either I have carried with me or that others have shared with me. Put a check mark beside every item on the list that could apply to you, as well.

_____ Poor people have poor ways; I might as well accept it.

_____ I'm really just not very smart.

_____ I'm just not as good as the people I'm competing with.

_____ I never come out on top.

_____ No matter how good things start out, something always ruins my efforts.

_____ I cannot really change; I just am who I am.

_____ I don't have the family background to be what I really want to be.

_____ I've never been able to do it before; why get my hopes up now?

_____ If I get too happy and relaxed, something will go wrong.

_____ If people knew how much of the time I was "faking it," I would really be in trouble.

_____ If I tried to change, it would just upset other people.

_____ It's selfish of me to spend so much time and energy on me.

_____ I don't deserve a second chance.

Now continue by writing below any other limiting beliefs that the list above brought to your mind. You can further add to the list by referring to the note card you began under "Erasing the Negative 'Tapes' " (page 47). The negative tapes you play in your head contain limiting beliefs that you are carrying around with you all the time. Identify every one you can find there, and add them to the list. Don't consider this list complete. Go on alert. Future challenges may bring more limiting beliefs to light. When that happens, write those down, as well. Ridding yourself of them will be a key step in your effective life strategy.

FRESHENING MY PERCEPTIONS

Acknowledging that you hold fixed beliefs about yourself, the people around you, and the world beyond you allows you to test and verify those beliefs. As a final reinforcement of Life Law #6—*There Is No Reality; Only Perception*—take an honest, heart-searching look at your fixed beliefs about yourself and each of the people or items below. Write down every fixed belief you hold in relation to every item on the "Limiting Beliefs" list you made in the prior assignment. Then create, in writing, a convincing counterargument to your current point of view. Think of it as a debate. You must write a winning counterpoint for every point. When you have finished with yourself, do the same for every person or item listed below. Then go back and force yourself to think of one more fixed belief under every heading. Remember, fixed beliefs become automatic. You'll have to work if you hope to root them out and rethink them.

Your mate
Fixed beliefs:

Alternative beliefs:

Your relationships with loved ones (You may want to add an extra page here to allow room for several people. Concentrate on those to whom you often react negatively.)
Fixed beliefs:

Alternative beliefs:

Your career
Fixed beliefs:

Alternative beliefs:

Your future
Fixed beliefs:

Alternative beliefs:

Your friends
Fixed beliefs:

Alternative beliefs:

God
Fixed beliefs:

Alternative beliefs:

The world in general
Fixed beliefs:

Alternative beliefs:

People in general
Fixed beliefs:

Alternative beliefs:

LIFE LAW #7   *Life Is Managed; It Is Not Cured*

Y*our Strategy:* Learn to take charge of your life and hold on. This is a long ride, and you are the driver every single day.

You've looked at your negative perceptions and limiting beliefs with the goal of replacing them with a constructive, reality-based point of view about your life. But that doesn't mean that you should now pretend that nothing in life is difficult or negative. Your life will include problems and challenges until it ends. Understand it, believe it, and accept it. Only when you do will you take Life Law #7—*Life Is Managed; It Is Not Cured*—to heart. Once you "get it," you'll see why it's essential that you learn to be an effective life manager in the midst of the challenges.

The following section will help you evaluate your life management performance and improve your ability to manage your life in the future so that you produce high-quality results. Do every exercise as thoroughly and honestly as you can. Your goal should be to acquire the skills you need to move beyond survival to success.

LIFE MANAGER PERFORMANCE APPRAISAL

I want you to take a step back and assess your life manager as objectively as you can. Disregard the fact that your life manager is you for the duration of this assessment. Intentions don't count. Neither do hopes. Focus on the results your life manager has produced in your present life. For each statement below, give your life manager a rating from 1 to 5 (1 = almost never, 3 = half of the time, 5 = almost always). Remember, as much as you sometimes wish you could, you can't fire your life manager. This assessment is a crucial first step toward working with, motivating, educating, and having patience with the only life manager you have—you.

_____ My life manager keeps me safe and secure from foolish risks.

_____ My life manager puts me in situations where I can utilize all of my skills and abilities.

_____ My life manager creates opportunities for me to get what I really want in this life.

_____ My life manager takes care of my health and well-being, physically, mentally, emotionally, and spiritually.

_____ My life manager selects and pursues relationships in which I can be healthy and flourish.

_____ My life manager requires me to reach and stretch for those things that will keep me fresh and young and alive.

_____ My life manager designs my day-to-day flow so that I enjoy some peace and tranquillity.

_____ My life manager arranges for some fun and recreation in my life.

_____ My life manager structures my world so that there is balance among those things I consider to be important.

_____ My life manager puts the most important things at the top of my "to-do" list every day.

_____ My life manager keeps me from taking on responsibilities that are rightfully someone else's.

_____ My life manager consistently puts my own urgent problems on project status.

_____ My life manager creates whatever situations or conversations are necessary to bring my problems and issues to closure.

_____ I am my life manager's most important client.

How does your life manager rate? The highest possible score is 70, and the lowest is 14.

CARE AND FEEDING OF MY LIFE MANAGER

One of the reasons your life manager may not be doing the job is that you haven't provided the necessary care and feeding. You've just assessed how well your manager is working for you. Now look at it from another angle. How well are you taking care of your manager? It's easy to deceive yourself in this area, so let's do a little reality check. For the next week, create an accurate record of the specific ways that you provide for your well-being.

Fill in the daily log provided on these pages, keeping track of what you do to actively provide for your physical, emotional, and spiritual health. List each activity and how much time you give to it. Include exercise, reading, recreation, meditation, involvement in religious observances, prayer, and self-improvement work of one kind or another. Don't exaggerate. Tell the truth. You can't change what you don't acknowledge.

	Physical what/how long	Spiritual what/how long	Emotional/Psychological what/how long
Sunday			

	Physical what/how long	**Spiritual** what/how long	**Emotional/Psychological** what/how long
Monday			
Tuesday			
Wednesday			
Thursday			
Friday			
Saturday			
Total Time			

Look closely at your record. Make adjustments for anything that is not typical of a normal week. Then look for areas that need improvement. List five areas for improvement. What are the pay-offs for not changing each? What might happen in each case if you did make a change?

1.

2.

3.

4.

5.

PUTTING MY LIFE ON PROJECT STATUS

Later in the workbook, you'll be creating a whole-life strategic plan that takes into account specific areas for improvement and how to put them on project status. In the meantime, take a trial run at being a more successful life manager.

Take the five areas you listed for improvement in the last

exercise and translate them into project-status action plans. ("I'll increase the time I allow for prayer from five minutes a day to fifteen." "I'll add a one-hour walk to my weekly routine." "I'll read that book I've been dying to read since last summer.") Write out your project-status goals below. For each one, spell out specifically what, when, and how. Identify the payoff for following through. After a week, come back to the list and record how well your plan worked. If it needs revising to make it more successful, do so. After another week, review it again.

1.

2.

3.

4.

5.

WEEK ONE REVIEW:

WEEK TWO REVIEW:

PLAYING THE "WHAT IF?" GAME

Fear has a positive function in human life, calling up the "fight-or-flight" instincts we need in times of real danger. But dread—the kind that grows out of unknown or worrisome possibilities—can chain you to a life you don't want. We play the "what if?" game—"Oh, what if I get fired?" or "What if Dad has a heart attack?" or "What if we end up divorcing?"—and ask the same questions over and over, because we never define the answer. The worries and fears that motivate the questions become un-respondable crises that hold us like quicksand. The only way to move beyond the eroding, paralyzing power of dread is to name your fears and claim responsibility for what you will do if the "worst" happens. When you turn the floodlight on and expose the monsters these "what ifs" become, you realize that the true consequences, however negative, are less horrific and more man-ageable than the vague terrors you sense but won't name.

With this in mind, play the "what if?" game with the goal of becoming a more effective life manager. In the space provided below, record twenty "what ifs" that represent the real, specific fears that wake you at night or preoccupy your precious waking hours. If your fears are often amorphous, force yourself to be more specific. Following each "what if" question, write at least one honest, real-world answer to the question. Make it your job to consider each fear seriously and comprehensively, and with foresight, describe in detail what would result and what you could do about it.

1 — What if . . . ?
Then

2 — What if . . . ?
Then

3 — What if . . . ?
Then

4 — What if . . . ?
Then

5 — What if . . . ?
Then

6 — What if . . . ?
Then

7 — What if . . . ?
Then

8 — What if . . . ?
Then

9 — What if . . . ?
Then

10 — What if . . . ?
Then

11 — What if . . . ?
Then

12 — What if . . . ?
Then

13 — What if . . . ?
Then

14 — What if . . . ?

Then

15 — What if . . . ?

Then

16 — What if . . . ?

Then

17 — What if . . . ?

Then

18 — What if . . . ?

Then

19 — What if . . . ?

Then

20 — What if . . . ?
   Then

An Inventory of My Life Decisions

Whether you consciously recognize it or not, you've already laid the foundation for the life management job you need to do. You've made some fundamental life decisions that can create order and clarity for the strategy you build and give you courage and commitment to face the difficulties. Right now, get in touch with those life decisions.

Remember, life decisions are those things that rise above passing thoughts or transient thoughts. Life decisions are those decisions that you have made at the core of your soul, that define who you are. They are not subject to renewed debate every day, or even every year. They are the fundamental values that define your life and its actions and patterns. You can make new life decisions, but you need first and foremost to recognize those that you have already made and determine whether you are living consistently with those life decisions.

Write down any and all of the life decisions that you are conscious of, and don't take anything for granted. To help you get started, read the checklist below, and mark any statement that describes one of your life decisions—convictions that you live by all of the time. Then continue the list until you've made a complete inventory of your life decisions.

_____ I will live with God in my family.
_____ I will live my life with integrity—meaning, specifically, that I will not lie and I will not steal.
_____ I will not fight in front of my children.

_____ I will not ask children to deal with or be burdened by adult problems.

_____ I will not resort to physical violence.

_____ I will take care of myself, so that I can take care of others.

Continue the list here.

What holes do you see in your list of commitments? What are the problems? Respond to your list here.

CLIMBING OUT OF THE COMFORT ZONE

The essence of Life Law #7—*Life Is Managed; It Is Not Cured*—is that you are your own best resource for a life that works. When you live in the comfort zone, you avoid risk and stay where you are simply because it is easier than changing. Maybe for you to climb out of the comfort zone, you will need to require more of yourself in terms of grooming, politeness toward others, exercise habits, or your own health management. Or you may need to exert more of your energy and ability in the direction of continuing your education or changing your job. The point is, to leave the comfort zone, which for many becomes a trap, you will have to avoid the temptation of doing what you do today, not because it's what you want to do, but because it's what you've gotten used to doing.

In the last exercise, you got in touch with the life decisions on which you are building your life, and you considered what needs to change. Now get practical about it. Take the time to focus on those things that you've identified for improvement of your management efforts. Then answer the question in writing below: "What am I resisting that I could do *today* to make my life better?" The answer to this will tell you where your comfort zones are. Remember:

> If you continue to do what you've always done, you will continue to have what you've always had.
> If you do different, you will have different.

LIFE LAW #8   *We Teach People How to Treat Us*

Your *Strategy:* Own, rather than complain about, how people treat you. Learn to renegotiate your relationships to have what you want.

By now, the knowledge you've been acquiring as you've read *Life Strategies* and worked through this workbook is adding up. You know that you are worthy of dignity and respect, but you also know that you create your own experience, for better or worse. It should come as no surprise to you when I say that you are responsible for the way people treat you. Before you can begin to fix what isn't working in your relationships, you will have to acknowledge your part in the problems. Only then will you be able to focus on the specifics of how you've taught people to treat you and pinpoint the response patterns you need to change.

You can create new "deals" in your relationships by re-quiring more of yourself and others, but you must begin with a solid understanding of what the current exchange really is. You must uncover the payoffs that keep you in relationships that don't work, and resolve to accept responsibility for changing.

The exercises that follow can put you on the right road if you commit yourself and do the work.

RELATIONSHIP QUESTIONNAIRE

Your life is almost certainly crowded with relationships, and the work you do now will apply to all of them. But the most meaningful relationships in your life have the greatest daily impact on you. They also provide a significant training ground for all the other relationships you sustain. For the purpose of putting first things first and creating change where it will make the biggest difference, use the following questionnaire to focus on your relationship with your "significant other." The questions may help you to diagnose not only the current status of your relationship, but the reasons for that status.

1—In all honesty, do you feel that you give, while your partner takes?   Yes No

2—Is your relationship a parent/child relationship, rather than the interaction of two adults?   Yes No

3—Do you and your partner fight with increasing frequency and/or intensity?   Yes No

4—Do you find yourself frequently apologizing?   Yes No

5—Do you feel that you just need some space and time alone?   Yes No

6—Looking back over the last year of your relationship, do you feel that you have made most of the sacrifices and changes?   Yes No

7—Do you find that you frequently make excuses for your mate, either to yourself or other people?   Yes No

8—Do you feel that your emotional needs are not being met?   Yes No

9—If you answered "yes" to #8: Do you feel that   **Yes No**
this has substantially cheated you out of a big
part of your life?

10—Are you physically frustrated in your relation-   **Yes No**
ship?

11—Do you feel that your relationship plays second   **Yes No**
fiddle to your mate's job, or the children, or
other priorities?

12—Do you keep significant secrets from your   **Yes No**
mate?

13—Do you feel that you are being used?   **Yes No**

14—Do you feel that there has to be more to your   **Yes No**
life than that which you are living in this relationship?

15—Do you see patterns developing or being   **Yes No**
played out in your relationship that mirror
those in either of your parents' marriages?

16—Do you find yourself too threatened to take the   **Yes No**
risk of true intimacy in your relationship?

17—Do you feel that you are the only one who   **Yes No**
legitimately works on your relationship?

18—Is guilt a major factor in your relationship?   **Yes No**

19—Do you feel that you are just going through   **Yes No**
the motions in your relationship?

20—Is your partner more like a roommate than a   **Yes No**
partner?

21—Do you entertain fantasies about not being in   **Yes No**
this relationship anymore?

22—Do you find that in order to have peace and   **Yes No**
harmony with your mate, you have had to stop
being who you really are?

23—Have you and your partner stopped working   **Yes No**
at your relationship, and just accepted it as is?

24—Are you in this relationship today simply be-   Yes No
cause you were in it yesterday, rather than because you really want to be?

Highlight those questions to which you answered "yes." The more "yes" answers you've given, the more trouble your relationship is in.

EVALUATING MY RELATIONSHIP

The quality of a relationship is a function of the extent to which it meets the needs of the two people involved. The questionnaire you just completed should give you valuable information about what is working and what is not in your most important relationship. Now use that information to take your diagnosis to a deeper level. What relational needs did you uncover as you answered the questions (your relationship may or may not be meeting them)? Identify at least twenty needs below. Be as thorough and honest as you can. To the right of each need you have identified, rate the degree to which you feel that the relationship meets that need. If it is substantially met in the relationship, give it 9 or 10. If it is not met at all, give it 1.

Need   *Rating*

1.

2.

3.

Need   *Rating*

4.

5.

6.

7.

8.

9.

10.

11.

12.

13.

	Need	*Rating*
14.		
15.		
16.		
17.		
18.		
19.		
20.		

Now let's translate the assessment exercise into a call for action. Add all 20 ratings together and divide the total by 20. We'll call this average rating your overall satisfaction with the relationship.

If your overall satisfaction rating is a 6, come up with four things that your partner can do to improve the relationship. Write them in the space below. If you gave the relationship an overall 2, come up with 8 things that your partner can do to improve the relationship. Whatever your rating, you need to articulate the number of improvements your partner can make that will bring your total to 10.

When you name those things necessary to bring your relationship up to a 10, make sure that they are things your partner can do something about. This is not an opportunity for criticism or simple inventory taking. This is your chance, for your sake and your partner's, to articulate a formula for success. Make the items action-oriented and make sure they describe what you want and need. Communicate them to your partner with clarity and specificity.

Now let your partner rate your relationship and then identify things *you* can do to bring your quotient to a total of 10. Again, it's important that your partner focus on things you can do something about. Each item should be expressed in terms of action you can take, and your partner should be careful that each action deals with what he or she wants and needs.

You have just created some significant talking points with positive potential outcomes for your relationship.

WHY I CHOSE YOU If you are in a significant relationship, something drew you to that person in the first place. More than likely, you could identify quite a few qualities, habits, or beliefs that formed the basis of your feelings and commitment. Right now, write a two-page love letter to your significant other. (Your partner is *not* allowed to read this!) In it, include a description of what it was that you saw in him or her that made you want to be in the relationship.

Be candid and specific. You were responsible for getting into the relationship. You need to understand why you made the choice.

From the letter you just wrote, list the valid reasons for choosing your partner.

Do those reasons continue to have validity? For example, if one reason you chose your partner is because he or she made you feel special, is that still the case? If not, this is another aspect of your relationship that you can work on. Mark it above and come up with at least one action your partner could take to restore that aspect to the dynamic of your relationship.

LET'S TALK ABOUT IT Remember that all the needs and problems you're identifying in this section have to do with Life Law #8—*We Teach People How to Treat Us.* If you have needs that are going unmet, if you experience deadness or loneliness in your relationship, if you receive less than the respect and dignity you deserve, you are responsible. One critical facet of teaching people a different set of rules in relation to you is your ability to communicate what you need and want.

Read the list of statements that follow. Put a check mark beside every statement that expresses an occasional (or frequent) problem on your side of the relational equation.

_____ I can't seem to find the right words to express what I want to say.

_____ I'm afraid that exposing myself will result in rejection.

_____ I'm not convinced it will help any to try to talk.

_____ I often don't talk because I'm afraid my opinion is wrong.

_____ I'm sometimes too angry to talk.

_____ Speaking up will only make things worse.

_____ I talk too much and don't give my partner a chance to speak.

_____ I lack good communication with God.

_____ I try to hide the truth.

_____ My speech is often defensive.

_____ I frequently bring up my partner's past failures.

_____ My actions don't match what I say.

_____ I don't really listen.

_____ I try to repay anger with anger or insult with insult.

_____ I tease my partner too much.

_____ I do not talk about really important things enough.

_____ I approach my partner with a general feeling of contempt.

_____ It is difficult for me to accept apologies or peace offerings once I am angry.

_____ If I am upset, I tend to withdraw or stonewall my partner.

_____ I escape into other people or activities rather than deal with my partner and our problems.

Every statement above describes self-defeating behavior that will stand in the way of reopening negotiations on your relationship. For each statement you marked, write down the payoffs that make that self-defeating behavior worth the losses to you.

Now write a brief paragraph in the space below outlining alternatives to each statement you marked.

MY LIFE For the sake of putting first things first, I had you work up until
NUCLEUS now on your relationship with your significant other. But you
have more than one important relationship in your life. I want
you to get in touch with who you consider to be the closest
people in your life. In the diagram below, put yourself in the
center circle. In the space within the circle around you, name
those you trust and value most in your life.

Keep this nucleus of relationships in mind as you do the next
exercise.

A SELF-INVENTORY

Turnabout is fair play. You've identified many ways in which you want the quality of your primary relationship to change. And you've focused on ways that your significant other can make positive steps in this regard. But you won't get far and you won't get cooperation until you see what your partner and others who are close to you have been letting *you* get away with. Have they taught you that it is okay for *you* to treat them with less than dignity and respect? Have they taught you that *you* can coast through your life, settling for less than your best? Do they let you walk away from a discussion about how you need to change?

Make a quick list of the fifteen most unhealthy behaviors that others have been letting you get away with in your relationships with them. For each of these behaviors, identify the payoff they have given you that has encouraged you to continue the negative behavior. Remember, you are accountable for a great deal of where your relationships are. Be willing to take this candid look at how you may be exploiting others in your relationships with them, whether by taking advantage of them or behaving abusively or insensitively toward them. To get you started, check any of the five behaviors listed below that you see in yourself. Then continue the list for yourself until you reach a total of fifteen.

_____ I become the problem to get my way.

_____ When I'm losing an argument, I change the game so I can win.

_____ I spread lies and gossip instead of dealing with a problem directly and honestly.

_____ I refuse to participate when I don't like what's happening.

_____ I play the nice guy rather than deal with conflict.

1.

2.

3.

4.

5.

6.

7.

8.

9.

10.

11.

12.

13.

14.

15.

Go back over the list you've just created. What would it take for you to change these self-defeating games? What can you do to give up each of the behaviors you've identified? Remember Life Law #5—*Life Rewards Action*. If you change, your relationships will change.

LIFE LAW #9   *There Is Power in Forgiveness*

Y*our Strategy:* Open your eyes to what anger and resentment are doing to you. Take your power back from those who have hurt you.

You've had some preliminary exercises in the business of teaching people how to treat you. But one of the easiest relational mistakes you can make is believing that you can only teach others when they "get it," too. Nothing causes more relational damage than the open wounds of unfinished emotional business— the bond of the negative emotions you feel—with somebody, somewhere. They died too soon. They don't accept that they're guilty as charged. They have no interest in your forgiveness. As a result, you tragically chain yourself to them through the unresolved hurt, anger, or hatred that you feel toward them.

This Life Law and the following exercises are based on the premise that forgiving those who have hurt us in our lives is first and foremost a gift to ourselves, and it does not depend on whether they deserve to be forgiven. If the object of your forgiveness receives a windfall when you set yourself free from the bonds of hatred, anger, and resentment, then so be it. You are worth it. Remember, forgiving someone does not mean that you have accepted what they did or that you intend to make yourself vulnerable to that person again. What it means is that you are unwilling to be controlled and dominated by this person by keeping the hurt alive with hatred and anger.

You don't have to remain stuck in the ugly world of negative emotions and so contaminate all the other relationships of your life. It's not an issue of whether the person who hurt you deserves your anger and resentment, but rather whether *you* deserve to be locked away behind the wall it creates. You create your own experience. You can claim the power of forgiveness and set yourself free. Don't bypass this essential work as your own life manager, or you'll rob yourself and the ones you love most.

ADMITTING THE WOUNDS

You can't change what you don't acknowledge, so clearly the first step for you to bring closure to the anger and resentment that are literally eating you alive is to get them out into the open. Right now, let the resentments that you carry rise to the surface.

Keep in mind that we sometimes protect ourselves at the conscious level by not admitting that we care about what someone did or didn't do in our lives. Even though we do not acknowledge it, however, we are still subject to the negative feelings and may be imprisoned by the pain. You must be willing to admit what has hurt you, what you have cared about, and what you have needed and did not get. Give yourself permission to acknowledge the hurts that you have suffered, even at the hands of those whom you love and respect the most. In order to "clean your house," you have to be willing to look in every nook and cranny. Honesty is never disloyalty.

What hurts against you or those you love can you "never forget"? List them below. After each item, describe how it has changed you—in other words, what carrying the negative emotion around with you has done to you. How has it changed how you relate to others?

PAYOFFS FOR THE NEGATIVE EMOTIONS

Now take each of the hurts you listed and apply Life Law #3—*People Do What Works.* You wouldn't accept the terrible consequences of holding on to your anger unless you perceived some kind of payoff. What is it? Does it give you an excuse to be unwhole? Does it allow you to keep other people at arms' length so you don't risk another hurt? Does it allow you to be "right"? For each of the hurts in the previous exercise, write a paragraph below that describes what you're getting out of choosing to let your negative emotions define your life.

BREAKING THE NEGATIVE BONDS

Each of the hurts you've listed and examined represents some person in your life, past or present, who has locked you in the bonds of hatred, anger, and resentment. I challenge you now to care enough about yourself and those you love to break that bond and be free of the tortured existence that comes from harboring those terrible emotions. Don't let even one of those who have hurt you win. Take the moral high ground. Give yourself what you deserve by forgiving them and freeing yourself from the emotional prison you've been living in. Transfer the names of each person from the prior exercises to this page. One name at a time, picture the person before you. Look him or her right in the eye, and read aloud the paragraph below. Repeat it in words of your own until you say it from the heart. Every time that person, and the hurt that has chained you together, comes into your mind, speak your freedom again. Repeat this process until you've truly freed yourself.

"You cannot lock me into a bond with you, where you become part of my very being and part of what I think, feel, and do every day. I will not bond with you through hatred, anger, or resentment. I will not bond with you through fear. I will not allow you to drag me into your dark world. By forgiving you, I am releasing me, not you. You must live with yourself every day. You must live with the darkness in your heart. But *I do not,* and I will not."

FORGIVING MYSELF

Negative feelings about yourself can cause as much damage as any bitterness you bear toward another person. I want you to root out any anger or hatred you carry toward yourself. On the page below, describe that thing in your life you feel most guilty about or ashamed of.

What was it?

How did it change you?

What has it done to the rest of your life and relationships as you carry it around with you?

Is there something you need to do, some reparation you need to make, to set the guilt aside? If so, what is it?

It may be too late to fix the source of your guilt. Have you taken the step of asking God's forgiveness? If God forgives you, do you have the right to waste the life you've been given in self-hatred? Describe the positive changes that can happen in your life when you climb out of the emotional prison you've been living in—for yourself, for the ones you love, for the world you contribute to.

PROUD TO BE ME Unresolved guilt feelings and self-loathing can blind you to all you are and have to offer. What are you most proud of about who you are? Check off any items that describe you in the list below. Then add to the list yourself. Write down any characteristic, quality, or achievement that gives you pride in being who you are. Remember, you can't give away what you don't have. If you don't love yourself, you won't be able to love others. If you don't forgive yourself, you won't be able to forgive others.

_____ I love deeply.
_____ I have achieved something very special.
_____ I have a great sense of humor.
_____ I have sacrificed for something or someone in a way that made an important difference.
_____ I take good care of my family.
_____ I have a good intellect.
_____ I have a way with children.
_____ I'm good in a crisis.
_____ I make a very good appearance.

Keep going. You haven't scratched the surface yet. Acknowledging all the good traits you have will be of enormous help in getting in touch with what you want.

LIFE LAW #10 *You Have to Name It to Claim It*

Your *Strategy:* Get clear about what you want, and take your turn.

This Life Law is probably the single most outcome-determinative factor in a successful life strategy. If you don't know what you want, you can't possibly plan how to get it, and as you've already experienced, it sure won't just fall in your lap. If you define what you want in terms that are too vague or general, you might as well not know. And if you define what you want incorrectly, you're going to go barreling down the wrong road and find yourself in a worse situation than where you started.

Remember, the most you'll ever get is what you ask for. Be bold. Be realistic. Be clear about the difference between what you really want and the means that may be just one of many paths to your goal. The exercises that follow may remind you of what you did in Part I of this workbook. Don't be fooled. You've learned a lot and worked hard on knowing yourself better since then. Use the ten Life Laws as you reconsider what you want and get ready to claim it.

WHAT I CAN ELIMINATE

Now that you've worked through the other nine Life Laws, you have a much better grasp of what you *don't* want in your life. Take a quick inventory, based on the exercises you've already completed in this workbook, and come up with thirty things you don't want to keep in your life any longer. Pay attention to unhealthy relationships, faulty assumptions, habits of denial and inertia, negative feelings and filters, and gaps in your knowledge. As always, be detailed and precise. No generalizations. No cop-outs. Just the truth about things that you want to eliminate from your life once and for all!

1.

2.

3.

4.

5.

6.

7.

8.

9.

10.

11.

12.

13.

14.

15.

16.

17.

18.

19.

20.

21.

22.

23.

24.

25.

26.

27.

28.

29.

30.

WHAT IS MY "BRASS RING"?

Imagine that I'm a genie, fresh out of the bottle. You have an unrepeatable opportunity to get what you want most in life, but on one condition: You have to be able to name what you want in such clear terms that I can't mistake what you're after. You are much better equipped now to answer this question than when you started this workbook. Give yourself time, when you have a full tank of energy, to work through the following questions. Follow the loop that takes you deeper and closer to what you really want as many times as it takes. Don't quit short of naming the goal accurately and specifically. (Refer to page 17 in Part I of the workbook and the example I give on pages 219 and following in *Life Strategies*.) Again, keep in mind that there is an important difference between the things that symbolize our deepest goals and the goals themselves. You want to get to the heart of what you want and need at this point.

1 — What is the "it" that you want?

2 — What will it look like when you have it?

3 — What will it feel like when you have it?

4 — What will you be doing behaviorally when you have it?

5 — Who are you doing it with?

6— Where will you be doing it?

7— How will your life be different from the way it is now when you have it?

8— What aspects of your life will you have to change in order to get it?

9— So what you really want is . . .

Fill in the blank in question #9 with the feelings you described in question #3, then go through the questions again. In the space below, note any answer that changes when you repeat the cycle based on the feelings you want to have. Push yourself to be more specific about how you want to feel.

Now repeat the process once again, and as many times as needed, working from the revised answer to question #3. Once you feel that you've nailed your brass ring, answer the following questions.

How will it look to people other than yourself when you get what you want? Describe yourself and your life from their point of view.

How will it make *you* feel about yourself?

What kinds of reactions and feelings will it generate in other people? Describe how they are likely to treat you.

What behavior will it involve for you?

OVERCOMING THE OBSTACLES

Go back to Part I and perform a scavenger hunt. Search for every last attitude, behavior, excuse, and negative emotion that could sabotage you when it's time to stand up and claim your victory. Create a laundry list right now of the obstacles you've thrown in your own path in the past, and resolve to acknowledge every one of them so you can begin to change them once and for all. To get you started, check off any of the items already listed if they apply to you, then add to the list until you've found every last obstacle you can.

To claim what I want, I will overcome my . . .

_____ comfort zone
_____ timidity
_____ negative tapes

_____ guilt

_____ tendency to play the victim

_____ feelings of inadequacy

_____ excuses

_____ self-consciousness

_____ tendency to fulfill my own negative thinking

_____ bitterness

_____ habits of self-defeating actions and attitudes

_____ laziness

_____ fear of failure

_____ parental legacy

_____ low standards

_____ fear of being selfish

Keep going!

WHAT MY SUCCESS WILL LOOK LIKE

As one final assignment before you move on to create your life strategy, I want you to write a letter to your life manager (you remember who that is). In the letter, spell out your life manager's job description in the coming process of touring your life in an organized way, creating your strategy, and finding a winning formula. Don't worry about the specifics of what you haven't done. Just give your manager a good working outline of what you expect: "Keep me at my task." "Organize my time so that I can give this the attention it needs and deserves." "Create the space for reflection that this will require." "Make sure I'm your number-one client." Be specific. You're closing in on the best outcome of your life. You don't want to quit before the race is run.

PART III

GET READY

Diagnosing Your Current Situation

Before you begin this portion of the *Life Strategies Workbook*, read Chapter 12, A Guided Tour of Your Life, in *Life Strategies: Doing What Works, Doing What Matters.*

By now you've become closely acquainted with the details of how you are living, what drives your attitudes and behaviors, and how you got there. You've also studied the ten Life Laws and begun to understand them specifically in the context of your own experience. You know that you chose your way to where you are, and the only way you'll move on is to choose differently. I haven't pulled any punches, and I sincerely hope that you've been just as honest with yourself as I have been with you.

You are now going to take an in-depth tour of your life using an organizational scheme that will allow you to see yourself more clearly and intimately than you ever have. On the pages that follow, you will be guided step by step to write out a detailed, multidimensional description of your life as it would be if it were ideal, and a mirror description as it actually is. Don't avoid the writing part of this process. You need to write it down if you want to effectively consolidate and use all the hard work you've done so far. Take it seriously. Take the time and effort needed to do this with utter honesty. Take it one step at a time through the assignments that follow, and I promise you that you will have the foundation laid for the most meaningful and exciting changes of your lifetime.

A GUIDED TOUR OF MY LIFE This process starts with a self-assessment of your life using the set of four formatted pages that begin on page 159 in this workbook. You'll need to have your book, *Life Strategies: Doing What Works, Doing What Matters,* open in front of you for the first two steps of the self-assessment. These pages provide a series of bulleted thoughts that you will complete under the appropriate headings on the formatted pages. You'll also need a red pen in addition to your regular blue or black pen.

Using one two-page blank chart for each of the Life Dimensions that make up your life, you'll answer the question, "Where am I currently, and what is it I truly want in this life?" The Life Dimensions fall under five categories—personal, relational, professional, familial, and spiritual—and include multiple facets. *You should perform a separate assessment for every dimension that applies to you under all of the five major headings.* For instance, you might begin with "Self-Esteem" under "Personal," "Objectives" under "Professional," or "Prayer Life" under "Spiritual." Choose whatever you want to work on first, but keep working until you've done them all. Use the Life Dimensions that follow, and add your own. By the time you have finished, you should have assessed somewhere between twenty-five and thirty Life Dimensions that together add up to a realistic, revealing snapshot profile of your life.

Personal Life Dimensions that you should assess include:

> Self-Esteem
> Education
> Finance
> Health

As you do these, refer to what you did in:

> "An Inventory of My Life Decisions" (page 113 of this workbook)

Relational Life Dimensions that you should assess include:

> Significant Other
> Friends
> New Relationships
> Repair of Existing Relationships
> Reestablishing Lost Relationships

As you do these, refer to what you did in:

> "Catching Up with the Ones I Love" (page 78 of this workbook)
> "An Inventory of My Life Decisions" (page 113 of this workbook)
> "Relationship Questionnaire" (page 117 of this workbook)

Professional Life Dimensions that you should assess include:

>   Job Performance
>   Business
>   Objectives
>   Promotions
>   Career Change

As you do these, refer to what you did in:

>   "An Inventory of My Life Decisions" (page 113 of this
>   workbook)

Familial Life Dimensions that you should assess include:

>   Parents
>   Children
>   Siblings
>   Extended Family

As you do these, refer to what you did in:

>   "An Inventory of My Life Decisions" (page 113 of this
>   workbook)

Spiritual Life Dimensions that you should assess include:

>   Personal Relationship with Your Higher Power
>   Your Spiritual Walk
>   Personal Study and Communion
>   Prayer Life
>   Life Focus

As you do these, refer to what you did in:

"An Inventory of My Life Decisions" (page 113 of this workbook)

Step #1: My Ideal Life Choose one specific Life Dimension to begin your assessment. The order is up to you. On the first assessment chart (page 159 of this workbook), write the name of the Life Dimension you've chosen in the blank at the top of the left-hand page. On this page, the bulleted questions on page 240 of *Life Strategies* will guide you through an evaluation of what this specific Life Dimension of your life would look like if it were a perfect "10." Before you begin filling in the page, refer to the assignments you've already completed in this workbook that pertain to the specific category and dimension you're working on. Remember, this is intended to describe your life—in *specific* terms—as you want it to be. Imagine ideal experiences in this Life Dimension— appearances, effects, emotions, relationships—as you work through the bulleted questions.

Step #2: My Actual Life When you have completed the "Ideal" page, move to the right-hand "Actual" page, and once again fill in the name of the Life Dimension. In the right-hand corner, rate your life as it really is in this dimension. Comparing your current situation with what you've just described as "ideal" should help you rate your "actual." If you see your life as perfect in this area, give it a 10. If it's a complete and total disaster, give it a 1. If you're feeling comfortable in this area, rate it a 5. Be completely honest with your rating. You can't change what you don't acknowledge. How you rate the specific Life Dimension will have an impact on how you develop your life strategy.

Next, use the bulleted questions on page 241 of *Life Strategies* to guide you through a complete and truthful description of how you're actually doing in this dimension of your life. Again, notice that for each of the five categories, I've suggested that you refer to certain assignments you've already done in this workbook. The former assignments include valuable information that you've already gathered and should help you to be specific and thorough as you complete Step #2.

As you complete this process, keep looking for answers to questions such as these:

> What characteristics am I carrying with me from one situation to the next?
>
> Do I go into situations expecting a negative outcome?
>
> Do I go into situations with a chip on my shoulder?
>
> Am I so judgmental that I condemn people in situations the moment I arrive?
>
> Am I so angry and embittered that I spew ugliness on everyone I engage?
>
> Am I so insecure that I look for and find examples of how I am mistreated in every situation?
>
> Am I so passive and unwilling to claim my space that I invite people to overlook and disrespect me?
>
> Do I hide insecurity behind a wall of false superiority and arrogance?
>
> Do I try so hard that I wear people out with my over-reaching?
>
> Do I spend all of my time comparing myself to others?
>
> Do I cheat myself out of genuinely experiencing situations by worrying the entire time about how people are viewing me?
>
> Have I doomed key relationships in my life by judging and condemning myself and others?

Put a bookmark in this page, and refer to the questions often. Knowing yourself is critical to the entire process of creating your life strategy. Writing out what you discover will give you added objectivity and keep you focused.

Step #3: Limiting Beliefs and Self-Judgments

Once you've completed both pages of the assessment for your first Life Dimension, go back and carefully read through your answers on the "actual" page. Using your red pen, draw a circle around every phrase you have used that expresses a limiting belief or negative self-judgment. You are looking for negative perceptions about yourself—who and what you are, and what you are capable of doing. This goes beyond stating what you have not yet accomplished in terms of character or action. It zeroes in on what you are assuming about yourself that puts you down, presupposes failure, or judges you with a harsh, unloving perspective. It's important that you capture every single instance in red ink.

Step #4: Obstacles I Must Overcome

The obstacles I'm referring to are the attitudes, emotions, or behaviors that block your path from your "actual" experience in this Life Dimension to the "ideal" you've described. Begin to develop an inventory of every obstacle by going back through the workbook and looking at what you wrote in these assignments:

"Erasing the Negative 'Tapes' " (page 47)
"What Needs to Change?" (page 56)
"The Rut Test" (page 74)

Extract every item you find that could impede your progress and write it in the Obstacle Inventory (Step #4—the third page of your assessment form) that follows the Life Dimension Chart.

Now think about your life circumstances, and write down any that obstruct your forward motion. These might include one or more of the following, or other things. If any on this list pertain to the particular Life Dimension, transfer them in writing to Step #4. Then add any additional items of your own.

Lack of money
A spouse who may undermine your confidence
Your living arrangements
Your lack of education
A debilitating physical challenge
Lack of time

Step #5:
Resources I Can
Put to Work
What have you got going for you that will help you move from your "actual" experience in this Life Dimension to the "ideal" you described? Refer to the following assignments that you've already completed in your workbook, and extract from them any resources that you currently have available to you. Write them on the Resources List for the Life Dimension you're working on (the fourth page of your assessment form).

"Hunting for the 'Gray Dogs' " (page 34)
"My Success Stories" (page 59)
"The Happiest Time in My Life" (page 71)
"My Top Twenty Achievements" (page 88)
"My Life Nucleus" (page 125)
"Proud to Be Me" (page 133)

The following list contains further examples. If any of these pertain to you, transfer them in writing to Step #5 of the particular Life Dimension you are considering. Then add any additional resources you can draw on in order to move from reality to your goal.

A supportive family
A good job
Intelligence
A clear resolve
Pain in the current situation
A realization that I have nothing to lose

Step #6:
My SUDS
(Discomfort)
Rating

At this point, I want you to step back and assess what you've done so far from a different angle. You've given your "actual" experience a numerical rating in comparison to the "ideal" rating of "10." Now ask yourself this question: "How much does this disparity bother me?" That is, how painful do you find the distance in this particular Life Dimension between the ideal and your actual life? Express your discomfort in terms of a number between 0 (no discomfort—"This is the way it is, but I could live with this for a long time to come") to 10 (unbearable pain—"I can't stand to live this way another hour"). Write the number down on the line provided on the fourth page of your assessment form.

Step #7:
My Motivation
for Change

As a final step in the assessment process, decide just how urgently you need to work on changing this Life Dimension. On pages 238–239 of *Life Strategies,* you'll find a detailed description of each of the potential priority ratings. Read each one carefully to see which best describes your sense of urgency for the Life Dimension you're working on. Then select one of the following and write it in the space provided on the fourth assessment page.

Urgent—change is of critical importance

High—change is worthy of serious focus

Medium—change calls for attention, but can wait while more urgent issues are addressed

Low—change would be desirable but may be of questionable relevance or import; not worthy of project status

LIFE DIMENSION ASSESSMENT FORMS

The following pages provide a four-page assessment form for you to use. You should make twenty-five photocopies of the form. Don't let that number intimidate you. If you have identified more than twenty-five Life Dimensions that pertain to your life, photocopy extra sets of pages before you start filling the forms.

Now work through the entire list of Life Dimensions on pages 148–150 of this workbook, one at a time, as well as any additional Life Dimensions you've identified for yourself. Distribute the work over a number of days so you can give focused, alert attention to each. You need to make a specific commitment to time, place, and duration. Do that here and now, in the space provided below. Don't fail to complete this essential part of the process, or you will have wasted what is probably your best chance at the life you want.

MY COMMITMENT TO COMPLETE THIS WORK

I will complete *all* of my Life Dimension assessments by _____. (Specify a date and time—be realistic, and follow through!)

In order to do this, I will do ____ (number) Life Dimension assessments a day at _____ (time of day) on the following days: _____ (dates).

Signed _____ Date _____

Life Dimension:_____   Ideal = 10

Step #1 If I was living my life as a "10" on this Dimension:

A—Behaviors:

B—Inner Feelings:

C—Negatives:

D—Positives:

Actual Self-Rating:_____ = (1–10)_____

Step #2: Since I am actually living this Life Dimension at level____:

A—Behaviors:

B—Inner Feelings:

C—Negatives:

D—Positives:

Step #3: Circle all judgments and limiting beliefs on the assessment chart for this Life Dimension.

Step #4: List here the obstacles you must overcome to move from "actual" to "ideal" in this Life Dimension.

Step #5: List here your resources for moving from "actual" to "ideal" in this Life Dimension.

Step #6: Rate your Subjective Units of Discomfort (SUDS) on a scale of 0 (no discomfort) to 10 (pain so intense that you cannot endure it one more day).

Why did you choose this rating?

Step #7: My motivation for change on this Dimension is (write one: Urgent, High, Medium, or Low). _____

SUMMARY OF PRIORITIES

The Summary Priorities chart following can help you arrange your priorities for change. This is an essential piece of the hard work you are doing, because it gives you a blueprint for action. It allows you to see what really deserves project status in your life today—what calls for immediate attention and action. In order to make the chart most effective and helpful, let's fill it in one step at a time.

First, go through all the Life Dimension Assessment Forms you've filled in and find every Life Dimension you have rated as "urgent." List them here.

Which of the items you listed is *most* urgent to you (your SUDS rating may be helpful at this point)? Put a 1 in front of that item. Put a 2 in front of the item that is most urgent of the remaining items in your list. Continue this evaluation until every item has been put in priority order. Then transfer the list in priority order to the "Urgent" column at right.

Now list and prioritize all the Life Dimensions that you rated as "high," and then transfer them to the "High" column.

Now list and prioritize all the Life Dimensions that you rated as "medium," and then transfer them to the "Medium" column.

Now list and prioritize all the Life Dimensions that you rated as "low," and then transfer them to the "Low" column.

SUMMARY PRIORITIES CHART

Urgent	High	Medium	Low

LIFE DIMENSION SUMMARY PROFILE CHARTS

Now create an overview of the hard work you've accomplished. On the following pages, you'll find five Life Dimension Summary Profile charts, one for each of the Life Dimension categories. On each chart, we've provided a continuum scale of 1 to 10 for each Life Dimension in that category, plus one for any Life Dimension that you added. These charts will allow you to compose an at-a-glance picture of the comprehensive assessment you just completed. They should give you a quick impression of what is working for you in your life and what is not. Again, this becomes essential as you plan your life strategy. It allows you to put first things first and address your most pressing needs with the greatest urgency.

First, select one of the category charts. On each Life Dimension continuum under that category, record your self-rating for that Life Dimension as of the time you filled out the assessment form. To do this, mark the numeral on the chart that corresponds to the rating you gave yourself.

After you have recorded the self-ratings for all the Life Dimensions in that category, add all of the ratings together and divide the total ratings by the number of individual Life Dimensions you recorded. This will give you an average rating for the entire category. Use this numeral for the "Overall Category Rating" continuum at the bottom of the chart.

Do this for all five categories, using the charts provided.

LIFE DIMENSION SUMMARY PROFILE
Category: Personal

Self-Esteem Rating

      1   2   3   4   5   6   7   8   9   10

Education Rating

      1   2   3   4   5   6   7   8   9   10

Financial Rating

      1   2   3   4   5   6   7   8   9   10

Health Rating

      1   2   3   4   5   6   7   8   9   10

_____ Rating

      1   2   3   4   5   6   7   8   9   10

Overall Category Rating

      1   2   3   4   5   6   7   8   9   10

LIFE DIMENSION SUMMARY PROFILE
Category: Relational

Significant Other Rating

       1   2   3   4   5   6   7   8   9   10

Friends Rating

       1   2   3   4   5   6   7   8   9   10

New Relationships Rating

       1   2   3   4   5   6   7   8   9   10

Repair of Existing Relationships Rating

       1   2   3   4   5   6   7   8   9   10

Reestablishment of Lost Relationships Rating

       1   2   3   4   5   6   7   8   9   10

_____ Rating

       1   2   3   4   5   6   7   8   9   10

Overall Category Rating

       1   2   3   4   5   6   7   8   9   10

LIFE DIMENSION SUMMARY PROFILE
Category: Professional

Job Performance Rating

       1   2   3   4   5   6   7   8   9   10

Business Rating

       1   2   3   4   5   6   7   8   9   10

Objectives Rating

 1 2 3 4 5 6 7 8 9 10

Promotions Rating

 1 2 3 4 5 6 7 8 9 10

Career Change Rating

 1 2 3 4 5 6 7 8 9 10

_____ Rating

 1 2 3 4 5 6 7 8 9 10

Overall Category Rating

 1 2 3 4 5 6 7 8 9 10

LIFE DIMENSION SUMMARY PROFILE
Category: Familial

Parents Rating

 1 2 3 4 5 6 7 8 9 10

Children Rating

 1 2 3 4 5 6 7 8 9 10

Siblings Rating

 1 2 3 4 5 6 7 8 9 10

Extended Family Rating

 1 2 3 4 5 6 7 8 9 10

_____ Rating

 1 2 3 4 5 6 7 8 9 10

Overall Category Rating

   1   2   3   4   5   6   7   8   9   10

LIFE DIMENSION SUMMARY PROFILE
Category: Spiritual

Personal Relationship with Your Higher Power Rating

   1   2   3   4   5   6   7   8   9   10

Your Spiritual Walk Rating

   1   2   3   4   5   6   7   8   9   10

Personal Study and Communion Rating

   1   2   3   4   5   6   7   8   9   10

Prayer Life Rating

   1   2   3   4   5   6   7   8   9   10

Life Focus Rating

   1   2   3   4   5   6   7   8   9   10

_____ Rating

   1   2   3   4   5   6   7   8   9   10

Overall Category Rating

   1   2   3   4   5   6   7   8   9   10

JUDGMENTS AND LIMITING BELIEFS

Now I want you to go back through all the Life Dimension Assessment Forms that you have created. Remember that Step #3 of the assessment process instructed you to find and circle in red every negative self-judgment and limiting belief that you included in your responses to the questions under A through D. Locate every circled item now, and copy it on this page to make a complete list of your self-judgments and limiting beliefs. This will give you an excellent overview of all that you are believing, and therefore being programmed by, that creates your negative internal dialogue.

WHAT I CARE ABOUT MOST

This crucial step will round out the work you've been doing in Part III of this workbook. Earlier, you prioritized specific changes that you want to make in your life. But in order for that to be meaningful in the larger picture of what your life will add up to, you need to put those specifics in the context of what you care about.

In the space provided below, I want you to list the top five priorities in your life. Begin by writing in the first space that which you hold to be the most important thing in your life. Then list the second most important thing, and so on. You may find it challenging to separate the relative importance of some of these items. Force yourself to order them nonetheless. Take the time to search your heart and be real about this.

Priorities   1.

2.

3.

4.

5.

HOW I USE MY TIME   This assessment will give you vital information as you move ahead toward creating a strategy that gives you what you most want from life. In the space below, list in descending order what it is that you spend your waking time on. Begin by subtracting the number of hours you typically sleep a night. Then figure out what activity or pursuit you spend the highest percentage of the remaining hours on, and write that in the first space. Continue in descending order, 2 through 5. When calculating work or family time, include the hours you spend traveling to and from work or school, or other events that have to do with that. Don't forget to honestly assess the amount of time you use for watching television, surfing the Internet, or playing computer games. If these use a significant amount of your leftover time, they could easily show up on your list. Be honest. Be accurate. Take nothing for granted. If need be, keep a log of your time for several days or a week to get a realistic evaluation.

Time Allocation   1.
Profile

2.

3.

4.

5.

THE THEMES IN
MY LIFE
By now, you may be feeling lost in the abundance of detail you've successfully brought together. In order to help you move back to the "big picture," I want you to review what you've recorded to see if you can identify certain recurring themes throughout. This will give you a better feel for where you are in your life and the kind of time frame you have for your goals. Begin this grounding exercise by responding to the questions below.

How wide is the gap between your actual adjustment and your desired adjustment? Are these levels of adjustment hugely divergent, or only mildly or moderately so?

Do your problem areas appear to be clustered in one or two categories of your life, or are they spread across the entire scope of your life?

What are the themes to your judgments and limiting behaviors? Are there consistencies in what you tend to say to yourself, no matter what the circumstances?

Are you riddled with self-doubt and/or self-loathing?

What emotions define you? Anger, fear, pain, or some other?

Are there major drains on your physical, emotional, or spiritual energy?

When you review your Summary Priorities Chart, do you detect parallels among those things you have put in the different categories? Are those things that you have listed as most urgent all in one category? If so, which category?

Do your priorities tend to involve other people, or are they largely or entirely focused on you?

What about time frames? Are your urgent priorities more short-term, or are they long-term?

Continue to look over what you've done and write down any further observations you have about the overarching themes of your life.

"ME IN THE FUTURE" This assignment requires that you imagine yourself in the starring role of your own life as you want it to be. Imagine that you have reached all your goals. You have "crossed the finish line" of what matters most to you. Describe your personality and behavior in terms of tone, mood, attitude, and texture. Describe what goes on inside your head *and* heart. Describe how you act when you're alone and when you're with other people. What do you look like? How do you feel? Write this as though you were talking about someone you are observing from the outside. Your life is a success. Tell me about the you who pulled it off. *This is an important part of building your life strategy. Do it well.*

PART IV

GET GOING

*Creating Your Strategy for
the Life You Want*

Before you begin this portion of the *Life Strategies Workbook,*
read Chapter 13, The Seven-Step Strategy, and Chapter 14, Finding Your Formula, in *Life Strategies: Doing What Works, Doing
What Matters.*

You've come a long, long way from where you were when you
started reading *Life Strategies: Doing What Works, Doing What
Matters.* You've taken a ruthlessly honest look at yourself and
taken responsibility for your life. You've given a significant amount
of time to studying the ten Life Laws and how they have shaped
and will continue to shape your experience. And you've conducted a thorough guided tour of your life that has put you in
a position of strength as you bring your progress in this book to
a close.

THE SEVEN STEPS You will now learn the seven key steps that will allow you to turn your dreams into goals. Because you know yourself and your life better than you ever have, you are equipped to develop a life strategy that allows you to change your life. You are in a unique position to discover and make the most of your personal winning persona. And you are ready to learn several critical aspects of living like a winner. You've made the choice to begin this odyssey, and you've made the choice to continue through the learning process. Take these next steps and let them create the positive momentum you want and need to alter your life forever.

Step #1: *Express your goal in terms of specific events or behaviors.* Go back to the Summary Priorities Chart on page 164 of this workbook. On that chart, you recorded every Life Dimension that you consider in "urgent" need of change. I want you to use the number-one Life Dimension on your "Urgent" list as your working example for the entire seven-step strategy.

The first step in turning this need for change into a realized goal requires that you express what it would take to reach your dream version of this Life Dimension in operational terms. "Operational terms" are descriptions that spell out all the details and aspects of the whole. Here's a simple example: I want to operationally define turning on a light in a room. To make it concrete and attainable, I have to include the following:

> Locate the switch that controls the flow of electricity to the light bulb.
> Approach the switch and grasp it between thumb and forefinger.
> Flip the switch up approximately one inch, listening for a distinct click.
> Release the switch and examine the light bulb to determine whether or not it is giving light.

I have now defined turning on the light in operational terms. Suppose that you have expressed as your goal "a happy, peaceful marriage." That's a fine goal, but it is not in operational terms. It needs to be broken down in just the way that I broke down the description of turning on the light. For instance, you might develop the description using the following:

> Do not scream and yell.
> Do not overly criticize.
> Express physical affection daily (hugs, kisses, an arm around the shoulder).
> Express love daily (say the words, "I love you," or otherwise communicate directly the depth of connection and caring).
> Express mutual appreciation for specific positive qualities in each other daily.
> Share the load of housework without resentment.
> Take time together to talk.

Make free time to spend apart for individual interests and
development.

And so on.

Return to the specific four-page assessment form you filled
out for this Life Dimension in the guided tour of your life on
page 157. Review the "ideal" description you created on the left-
hand page. Then identify what you want, and write it in the
space below.

Now push yourself to express what you want in even more specific terms. Answer the following questions. Be concrete. Include
precise details. Don't stop until you have a solid, proactive definition of your goal for this particular Life Dimension.

**What are the specific behaviors or operations that make up the goal?
In other words, what will I be doing or not doing when I am "living
the goal"?**

How will I recognize the goal when I have it?

How will I feel when I have it?

My goal, expressed in operational terms, therefore, is this:

Step #2: *Express your goal in terms that can be measured.* You now have an operational definition of your number-one priority for change in your life. The next step requires that you express your goal in measurable outcomes. You must be able to tell whether you're moving closer to your goal, how far you still have to go to reach your goal, and how you will recognize the goal when you have achieved it. Only *you* know the circumstances, relationships, behaviors, and emotions that achieving your goal will involve. It's up to *you* to make all of these aspects clear to *you*. Otherwise, you will derail your progress before you even get on the tracks.

Perhaps you realize that for your marriage to grow, for example, you need to relocate farther away from your parents or your spouse's parents because their interference or influence has had an adverse effect on what you and your partner are trying to build together. Maybe you see now that the business environment you've made yourself a part of is the wrong one for you, and you need to move into another field to find a better fit. Or possibly, you recognize that your life is badly out of balance in terms of the proportion of time you give to health-enhancing recreation, and you need to eliminate a specific amount of nonproductive TV time to allow more exercise and attention to physical well-being. All of these sorts of descriptions should be expressed in terms of what you will be able to measure as success. "Move to a house that is at least a 45-minute drive from the in-laws." "Replace my current job with a new job in a different field (be sure to specify which field)." "Watch no more than one half-hour of television a day, and spend at least five hours a week walking and jogging." Now your goal has become something specific you can do, rather than something vague with no way to recognize if you have achieved it or not.

Answer the following questions using specific, concrete, detailed language that nails every term or adjective you have included in your goal.

In order for your goal to be achieved, where would you be located?

In order for you to reach your goal, who would you be with?

How much money would you have?

In what type of work or activities would you be involved?

How would you behave?

How much time would you spend doing certain activities?

Now create five additional questions that pertain to the details of the goal you expressed, and answer them in measurable terms, as well.

1.

2.

3.

4.

5.

My goal would include the following measurable outcomes:

Step #3: *Assign a time line to your goal.* In order for your goal to become a reality, you must assign a particular schedule or calendar for achieving it. When you force yourself to put your goal on a time line, you effectively impose project status on it. Because you have a deadline, you feed the sense of urgency that will impel you forward, and, at the same time, you forestall inertia and procrastination.

Begin by assigning a due date for your number-one priority goal.

Next, work backward from your due date to determine the midpoint of the time span you have to accomplish your goal. Suppose, for example, that your child wants to have an A average at the end of the first six weeks of school. The time line is easy since the target date is six weeks away. The goal is measurable because the quantifiable result will be expressed in A grades. What are the intermediate steps? Perhaps in this case, the child would divide the process into week-long intervals. At the end of each week, he or she would assess the graded work accomplished, then average the grades or ask the teacher for the current status. If his or her average falls below "A," the child has to make interim adjustments—he or she must spend additional study time to enhance performance, as opposed to waiting until the six weeks are up and realizing he or she had missed the goal.

The same holds true if you want to lose forty pounds of extra weight. How much time will it reasonably take in total? If you give yourself four months to lose the weight, you might decide to check your progress against the goal every two weeks. An even weight loss would require that you lose five pounds every two weeks. If you don't, you should be motivated to change some aspect of your weight-loss plan to make it more effective, including changing your behavior so it is harder for you to "cheat." By midpoint (two months), you would want to be down twenty pounds.

Answer this question: "Where do I have to be by the midpoint of my schedule in order to reach my goal in the time I've allotted?" Describe this intermediate stage with the same level of detail you used to give an operational, measurable definition of your goal in the first place.

Step #4: *Choose a goal you can control.*

By now, you may be running into some difficulty with the goal you developed from your number-one priority for change. If so, this step will almost certainly explain why. There are some aspects of life that we simply cannot control: the weather, the state of the world economy, the behavior of strangers, the mood of that troublesome relative. Your goals need to be based solidly in the real world of what you *can* change and affect. Test the goal you're presently developing for this critical quality. If you need to, adjust it now so that it truly represents what you can do. Then rewrite it in the space below.

Step #5: *Plan and program a strategy that will get you to your goal.*

You've identified your goal in highly specific terms. You've established a time frame that puts your goal on project status. And you've tested your goal for whether it actually falls within your control. Now you need to do some creative programming to pave the way for success. Specifically, you need to program your *environment*, your *schedule*, and your *accountability*. When your enthusiasm flags and your willpower conks out, you need to have these three elements programmed in such a way that they support you.

Let's start with your environment. Realistically assess the obstacles that have an impact on reaching the goal you've chosen. This means anticipating the times, places, circumstances, events—even people—that typically make it difficult for you to stay the course and finding a way to manipulate the parts they play in your life.

Begin by making a comprehensive list of every element in your life that could get in the way of reaching your goal. To help you thoughtfully look for every possible obstacle, review the assignments you completed for Part I. In addition, look at the following:

"What Did *I* Do?" (page 45)
"Where Was *I* When That Happened?" (page 46)
"What Needs to Change?" (page 56)
"My Success Stories" (page 59)

Now make your list of obstacles. Leave a space after each item.

Once you have completed the list, go back and identify the pay-offs that have allowed these obstacles to stand in your way in the past. To take the bite out of each obstacle, what can you do, change, or arrange?

Step #6: *Define your goal in terms of steps.* Step #5 deals with your environment, eliminating or defusing anything that will set you up for failure, and incorporating as much as possible everything that will support your goal. Now let's talk about schedule.

You've already set your goal and identified a specific mid-point on your time line for change. In order to effectively set and maintain your schedule, you need to create a realistic strategy that breaks your goal into measurable steps. It could be that when you work backward from your desired outcome, you discover that the time frame you decided on is impossible—you've already doomed yourself to miss your deadline. Or you may find that you could reach your goal much sooner than you realized. You won't know until you get real about what you need to do, step by measurable step.

Do that now. First, in the space below, describe the specific steps that you will have to take in order to reach your goal. Think of it as writing a recipe or an instructional guide. Name each step in terms of action and intermediate outcome. In other words, what will it look like when that step is completed? How will you know—concretely—when you've accomplished the step? Don't leave anything out, or it may not *turn* out.

Next, assign a reality-based time frame to each step. Remember that your goal is on project status—and it's at the top of your "Urgent" list. Assign no more and no less time than the step should realistically take. Finally, fill in the time-line grid provided below. Above the line, describe each step in terms of your action. Below the line, write the actual date by which you will have completed that step. You have now defined and scheduled your path from where you are now to where you will be when your goal is reached.

ACTION:

DATE COMPLETED:

Step #7: *Create accountability for your progress toward your goal.*

One of the reasons why you haven't met important goals in the past is that you let yourself get away with not doing what was needed *when* it was needed. You failed by degrees, falling further and further short of the outcome you wanted. Choose different behavior this time, and you will choose a different outcome—success!

You've programmed your environment and your schedule. The final step in turning your dreams into goals requires that you make yourself accountable throughout the steps toward your goal. This means enlisting someone who will serve as a "teammate," someone to whom you commit to make periodic reports. In other words, choose someone from among your family and friends to whom you will have to confess if you fail to do what you plan to do.

Before you go any farther, refer to "My Life Nucleus" on page 125 of this workbook. When you completed the circle, you identified your relational network of support. This may very well be your greatest resource now, as you take the seventh step toward reaching your goal.

Answer the questions that follow to help you set up a meaningful, effective accountability system.

Who among your family and friends would be the most effective teammate for this specific goal? For example, who would most strongly support what you want to accomplish? Who would be available and willing to act in this capacity? Who could provide support without bringing unhealthy relational baggage along?
NAME:

How often do you need to report on your progress in order to stick with it? Daily? Weekly? Quarterly? This will depend on the specific goal and how long the intervals are between identified steps. If the goal involves ending compulsive behavior, you could very well need a daily report.

FREQUENCY:

What precisely do you intend to report? How will you measure whether you are on target or not? It's important that you communicate this clearly to your teammate so that he or she knows what you need to accomplish at each stage toward your goal.

NATURE OF ACCOUNTABILITY:

As a final action in preparation for this step, set a time by which you will secure someone to whom you can report.

DATE TO BEGIN:

CREATING THE MOMENTUM OF SUCCESS

You now have a working knowledge of exactly what you need in order to build a strategic plan for your life. You have begun the process by putting one of your Life Dimensions on project status and applying the seven-step strategy. Understand that once you create a proactive strategy for your life and take the first baby steps in that direction, you pave the way for more and more success.

Plan to further that momentum of success right now. Go back to your Summary Priorities Chart (page 164) and your Life Dimension Summary Profiles (pages 165). You have assessed your life under five major headings, or "life strands." Use your assessment summaries to set a particular goal in each of the life strands. You will, in effect, plan to put five Life Dimensions on project status, which will allow you to begin changing your life one step, one goal, one priority at a time. Then fill in the following pages, one for each goal, to map out your seven-step strategy for each. If you have any questions about what any step requires, review the detailed pages you have just completed for your number-one priority.

Life Dimension: _____

Step #1: Express your goal in terms of specific events or behaviors.

Step #2: Express your goal in terms that can be measured.

Step #3: Assign a time line to your goal.

Step #4: Choose a goal you can control.

Step #5: Plan and program a strategy that will get you to your goal.

Step #6: Define your goal in terms of steps.

Step #7: Create accountability for your progress toward your goal.

Life Dimension: _____

Step #1: Express your goal in terms of specific events or behaviors.

Step #2: Express your goal in terms that can be measured.

Step #3: Assign a time line to your goal.

Step #4: Choose a goal you can control.

Step #5: Plan and program a strategy that will get you to your goal.

Step #6: Define your goal in terms of steps.

Step #7: Create accountability for your progress toward your goal.

Life Dimension: _____

Step #1: Express your goal in terms of specific events or behaviors.

Step #2: Express your goal in terms that can be measured.

Step #3: Assign a time line to your goal.

Step #4: Choose a goal you can control.

Step #5: Plan and program a strategy that will get you to your goal.

Step #6: Define your goal in terms of steps.

Step #7: Create accountability for your progress toward your goal.

Life Dimension: _____

Step #1: Express your goal in terms of specific events or behaviors.

Step #2: Express your goal in terms that can be measured.

Step #3: Assign a time line to your goal.

Step #4: Choose a goal you can control.

Step #5: Plan and program a strategy that will get you to your goal.

Step #6: Define your goal in terms of steps.

Step #7: Create accountability for your progress toward your goal.

Life Dimension: _____

Step #1: Express your goal in terms of specific events or behaviors.

Step #2: Express your goal in terms that can be measured.

Step #3: Assign a time line to your goal.

Step #4: Choose a goal you can control.

Step #5: Plan and program a strategy that will get you to your goal.

Step #6: Define your goal in terms of steps.

Step #7: Create accountability for your progress toward your goal.

FINDING MY FORMULA   You've reached the final stage of preparation for creating a personal life strategy. You have already uncovered the traits, tools, and characteristics with which you came equipped in the first place. To that you've added awareness, know-how, focus, and clarity. And you've brought to bear your motivation, intelligence, and sense of need. Now tune in to several aspects of being a winner in this world.

Begin by embracing your unique persona to get the most out of your life. Your "formula" will include whatever attitudes, intensities, behaviors, and characteristics make up your peak performance—your "zone." No one can give this to you; you're one of a kind. You need to answer the question: "Based on results, what aspects of being who I am and what I am work?"

Remember that there is no right or wrong here. You are looking for what works, not what is "right." Have fun with this. You are a unique individual, and whatever style works for you is acceptable. Give yourself permission to turn who you are into positive results. But first and foremost, claim who you are, immerse yourself in it, and allow yourself to be at your peak of effectiveness.

To help stimulate your thinking, respond to each of the following questions.

1 — Do you do your best when you are self-assured (even cocky) or when you are quiet but determined?

2 — Is high energy your deal, or is yours a more methodical, persistent style?

3 — Are you best when you take charge, or are you a strong supporter?

4 — Is a positive, receptive attitude your best mode, or do you need to maintain a healthy skepticism?

5 — Are you a loner or a team player?

6 — Do you shine as the idea person, or do you make your best contribution in concretely fulfilling the ideas of the theorists?

7 — Is in-the-spotlight performance your strength, or are you an ace behind-the-scenes person?

8 — Do you do your best as an encourager or as an analyst?

9 — Are you a good juggler or do you thrive upon concentrating on one intense focus at a time?

10 — Do you deal well with high-stress situations, or does a more even-keeled scenario bring out the best in you?

In the space below, write a character sketch of yourself at your most effective, describing your attitudes, energy, relational style, and spirit as they feel and appear when you're in the "zone."

LEARNING FROM MY MISTAKES

If it's not working, don't persist in it, whatever it is. But how do you discern what is not working? By the outcomes you do not want. Return to the extensive self-assessment you have accomplished throughout this workbook. You have chosen to take responsibility for every mistake you've made (review Life Laws #2, #4, and #8, *You Create Your Own Experience, You Can't Change What You Don't Acknowledge,* and *We Teach People How to Treat Us*). You have identified more than enough mistakes on these pages to keep the learning curve steep for some time to come. And chances are you haven't made your last mistake yet.

As a practice run, turn to the Life Dimension assessments that you completed in Part III of this workbook. Find the particular assessment(s) out of the twenty-five to thirty assessments that you completed that you rated the highest on the SUDS scale—indicating that the degree "off perfect" of this Life Dimension causes you the greatest discomfort. If you ranked more than one Life Dimension at whatever your highest ranking was, choose the one of greatest urgency to you. Now answer the following questions as thoroughly and honestly as you can. Consider it "Mistake Academy." Don't deny or ignore your mistakes; make them work for you. Remember, you can't change what you don't acknowledge. Let this be part of your training ground for a winning personal formula.

What went wrong in this Life Dimension?

What specifically did I do or fail to do to create this painful reality?

What could I have done differently that would have produced a different outcome?

In what particular ways might the outcome have changed?

How, in measurable, precise terms, can I avoid this mistake in the future?

LEARNING FROM MY SUCCESSES

You've made your mistakes, but you've also made some effective choices. The things that are going right in your life are going right because you made them go right.

Return to the Life Dimensions chart on page 230 of *Life Strategies: Doing What Works, Doing What Matters.* Let the chart serve as a spur to your thinking. What can you identify in each of the five life categories that is working for you? For example, you may have devised an excellent way for the entire family to be actively involved in the business of housework. The instincts, skills, and sensitivities that you put to work to find a productive, peaceful way for all to participate are resources that can be applied elsewhere. Remembering how you planned, what you put into the ongoing process, and what you have learned about yourself and your family members can serve you. Identify what things are working in your life. Write them below.

PERSONAL:

RELATIONAL:

PROFESSIONAL:

FAMILIAL:

SPIRITUAL:

For each success that you've identified, answer questions such as those that follow. If you've created success once, you can create success again. If you've created success in one Life Dimension, you can create it in others.

What specifically is working in this relationship, situation, or circumstance?

What choices have I made in the past to produce this outcome?

What do I continue to do in this area that contributes to its success?

Which of my positive qualities come into play? Why?

What characteristic behaviors of mine are working in this area?

What attitudes do I bring to it?

What is different in this area from other areas in which I am not enjoying such success?

SUCCESS STUDY: THE TEN KEY ELEMENTS

Take this final assignment and practice it until it becomes a habit. It is a primary tool for successful living. As you observe and assess the successful people who come to your attention, you'll be gleaning valuable information that you can incorporate into your own personal life strategy.

Turn to pages 274–278 in *Life Strategies*. Read the descriptions of the top ten elements that are consistently present in the successful people I have studied. Then start an investigative search of your own. For every element, find one person in your own life or in the public eye who exemplifies that quality. Describe some particular aspect of the result that the quality is creating in the person's life. Then identify some specific area of your own life in which you would make a needed change if you would incorporate the quality.

For example, suppose that the librarian in your town has exhibited a very clear vision of what he or she wants to accomplish for the literacy of the children in the community. The librarian has communicated the goal clearly to the town and has developed a series of free programs—"readathons," story-telling events, essay contests, and so forth—that serve that goal. As a result, the children have indeed become more interested and active in reading and writing. The town has coalesced around a worthy goal, and the librarian is legitimately proud and satisfied. You can learn from the librarian that knowing and articulating a specific agenda, doing focused research, and developing specific strategies, regardless of the hard work, reaps appreciable benefits that extend to others. Because the librarian could "see" the end result, the plan was energized and cohesive.

The idea here is to incorporate behaviors and attitudes that lead to success. Observation can be a great teacher. You're not trying to be someone else, but rather letting their successful behavior patterns instruct your own personality and style.

Vision   SUCCESSFUL PERSON:
Life result:
How my life could benefit:

Strategy   SUCCESSFUL PERSON:
Life result:
How my life could benefit:

Passion   SUCCESSFUL PERSON:
       Life result:
       How my life could benefit:

Truth   SUCCESSFUL PERSON:
       Life result:
       How my life could benefit:

Flexibility   SUCCESSFUL PERSON:
       Life result:
       How my life could benefit:

Risk   SUCCESSFUL PERSON:
       Life result:
       How my life could benefit:

Nucleus   SUCCESSFUL PERSON:
       Life result:
       How my life could benefit:

Action   SUCCESSFUL PERSON:
Life result:
How my life could benefit:

Priorities   SUCCESSFUL PERSON:
Life result:
How my life could benefit:

Self-management   SUCCESSFUL PERSON:
Life result:
How my life could benefit:

Now go back to your number-one priority for change, and identify the ways in which these elements should be present in the strategy you have developed. Consider ways in which you can begin to make each of them more a daily element in *your* life.